Bearing Up

THE REMARKABLE SURVIVAL OF
THE LANDED ESTATE

Bearing Up

THE REMARKABLE SURVIVAL OF
THE LANDED ESTATE

FRANCIS FULFORD

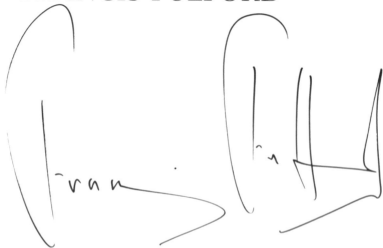

Timewell
Press

First published in Great Britain in 1998 by
Timewell Press Limited
8 Balham Hill, London SW12 9EA

ISBN 1 85725 137 7

Typeset by Antony Gray
Printed and bound in Great Britain by
MPG Ltd, Bodmin, Cornwall

Acknowledgements

Over the years I have picked the brains of many leading land agents, landowners and agricultural economists, frequently over heavily liquid lunches at their expense. It is difficult, therefore, because of the alcoholic haze which obscures memory, to single out individuals for thanks. I have also been the beneficiary of much erudite and interesting research, in particular from Savills, Strutt & Parker and Bidwells, but also from many other members of the estate-agent fraternity. Without this constant stream of information I would not have been able to write my monthly article for *The Field*, let alone this book.

However, this book would never have been written without the long-term support and encouragement of the editors of *The Field* magazine, who have put up with my idiosyncratic ways for the best part of ten years and provided me with a column in which to publish my views on farming, the property market, the heritage industry and indeed on most of the issues which concern the countryside today. I have, naturally, drawn heavily on material I have contributed to them over the years in writing this book, so if the odd reader thinks a phrase, or an idea, has a familiar ring, then it is probably because he has already read it in *The Field*.

Lastly my thanks are due to my long-suffering wife who, on the whole, has left me alone to get on with writing rather than pestering me to carry out those quantities of tedious domestic chores that beset us all.

Contents

	Introduction	9
1	*History*	11
2	*The Big House*	23
3	*The Big House – the Public Sector*	51
4	*The Contents*	62
5	*The Park and Gardens*	72
6	*The Land*	76
7	*Scotland*	104
8	*The Common Agricultural Policy*	115
9	*The Woodlands and Forestry*	127
10	*Forestry – the State Sector*	143
11	*Diversification*	148
12	*Houses and Villages*	153
13	*The Family*	165
14	*The Professionals*	173
15	*Field Sports*	179
16	*The Church*	190
17	*Designations*	196
18	*The Future*	200

Introduction

I seem to hear a groan going up – 'Oh no, not yet another book on country houses and estates! How boring.' Well, boring is one thing I hope this book is not. As for 'yet another book . . . ', it is true that in recent years a veritable avalanche of publications, not to mention TV documentaries, has been produced on the subject. Reading or viewing these has given me an inkling of what it must be like to be a gorilla in a zoo, stuck behind bars and observed all day by experts, or, alternatively, pursued by the self-same experts in one's jungle fastness. They are, sometimes, well researched and lucidly written, but their conclusions are all too often so much garbage. The reason is, of course, that they are not written by a gorilla. Well, this book is.

The end result of all this mass of publicity is that there has probably been more rubbish talked and written about the countryside of Britain in general and about country houses and estates in particular, than about any other single topic; this book will try to set the record right.

In short, that is the reason for this book. I am bored by people talking and writing on something called the environment when what they really mean is the countryside. I am equally bored by experts pontificating on the subject of the so-called National Heritage when what they mean are people's private homes, and I am particularly bored by a Parliament which is packed with lawyers, bankers, social workers and the like caving in to every urban-based pressure group with a bee in its bonnet about rural affairs.

What else bores me? Being patronised by the self-same groups of people who seem to think that because one lives in the country one is thick (or, as they would probably say, mentally challenged); having to read page after page of close-typed rubbish written by people without the faintest ability to write English and whose knowledge of the subject they purport to be expert on is infinitesimal but who are paid to churn out reports (like the last government's White Paper on Rural Affairs); and having to listen to the leaders of many organisations which represent rural-interest groups as they grovel to some of the above people in the hope of getting some crumbs from the taxpayers' table; these are just some of the things which irritate me and have inspired me to put pen to paper. There are many others, as you will see.

I make no apologies for discoursing on the history of how great landed estates evolved and why so many have disappeared over the last hundred years, since, until the 1920s, the landed estate to all intents and purposes *was* the English countryside, just as the Scottish estate still is – by and large – the dominant factor in the Highlands of Scotland. I will argue that landed estates throughout Great Britain have been a force for good in the countryside and the problems of the countryside today are chiefly attributable to a misguided vendetta waged against them over a span of a hundred years.

I have attempted to set out the reasons for the demise of so many estates since the turn of the century, and have tried to draw lessons from the mistakes our ancestors made, with the aim in so doing of helping to ensure future generations don't fall into the same traps. In short, this book contains, among other things, a 'survival guide' for estate owners.

This book is not designed for scholars (though some may benefit from reading it) or politicians (though they would undoubtedly benefit from reading it) but for the general public. I am fully aware that the subject of every chapter could in itself make a lengthy book but my purpose is to provide a quick and, I hope, amusing overview of how the countryside has developed and is still developing and of the role played by the country estate in that development.

CHAPTER 1

History

The history of England is emphatically
the history of progress.

LORD MACAULAY

OK, let's begin at the beginning – which for the purposes of land ownership and country houses is 1066. To understand the present, a knowledge of history is a great asset and nowhere is this more true than in arriving at an understanding of the reasons behind the buildings, parks and landscapes which today still astonish the eye.

We all know, because we used to be taught such matters in school, that William the Conqueror introduced the feudal system to this country after he won the Battle of Hastings. The basis of feudalism was the possession of land and in essence it was a simple and logical concept.

In effect, after he won the battle, all land in England became the personal possession of the king. That was fine in theory but in practice he needed to be able to control and rule that land and for that purpose he needed men, i.e. soldiers. Soldiers need paying otherwise they get restless and don't perform. The king, like virtually all kings throughout history, was short on cash but long on land. So the simple solution was to pay them in land in return for certain basic duties.

Accordingly, the king's best and most trusted companions received large chunks of England. They too were then confronted with the same problem which had beset the king, so they, in turn, divided up their estates among their own followers in a like manner. The smallest area of land given was a manor, which varied in size and wealth but was on average about eight hundred acres. Later each manor came to be assessed in terms of a knight's fee. Rich manors might be worth a whole knight's fee, poor ones only a fraction of one. In essence it meant that a manor worth one knight's fee could put into the field one armoured knight and his necessary retinue. Each layer of the feudal system swore an oath of loyalty, or homage, to the man who had given them the land and agreed to provide him with a certain number of armed men on specific occasions. The end result was that William managed to reward all his followers and ensure, in theory, that all England was held by men loyal to him; thus his writ ran throughout his realm and gave him a cheap army to call upon should the occasion arise. A neat, simple solution to a complex problem – providing, of course, everyone obeyed the rules and abided by their oaths.

The theory of feudalism was good and in line with the latest teachings in all the most modern business schools. In practice, of course, there were severe faults to it. Yet under a strong king it worked. A Saxon chronicler wrote, on William's death, that 'any honest man could travel across his kingdom without injury with his bosom full of gold'. This is more than can be said in our current democracy; perhaps we should return to feudalism? It is not the purpose of this book to look into the practical effects of feudalism or how it worked, but a word must be said about how the system evolved in the first place and why the ownership of land was so important.

The concept of a warrior class or race is probably as old as time. It is fair to say that some people like to grow things and live in peace with their neighbours while others want to biff their neighbours on the nose. Even today when we are all meant to be peace-loving traders whose only concern is whether we can make enough money to buy a better car, there is a sizeable minority among us who would prefer to be crossing the channel and carrying out some rape and pillage in France rather than taking a day trip on the ferry and paying our Gallic neighbours for goods which our ancestors took by force of arms.

Warriors though are not necessarily stupid, and most of them could work out the simple economics that however much fun raiding your neighbours was it made you considerably richer if you could enjoy some form of peace and stability on your own patch. Those of your peasants who ploughed the fields and worked the land would be able to pay you bigger rents if they were left to get on with the job in hand and, with the money raised, the warrior could equip a bigger raiding party for his autumn holiday spree.

If warriors are not stupid, neither were the humble men of the land and they could see the logic of effectively paying for their defence by having a strong lord who could ensure that they were left alone to lead their lives in relative peace. In other words, the system was symbiotic in its true sense. Logic also dictated that as the lord of the manor had so much to lose if he was on the losing side he would fight hard in any battles against invading forces in order to protect his revenue base, i.e. his tenantry.

Of course, things often went dramatically wrong, as when the Saxon thanes went off to fight at Hastings and lost. Then new landlords appeared hotfoot from the battlefield to take over the defeated landlords' manors. But because the Normans' aims were those of conquerors and not those of raiders they left the Saxon peasantry, with some exceptions, unmolested, and allowed them to continue to farm the land. Interestingly, the Normans also appear to have been avid agricultural reformers: the Domesday Book of 1086 is littered with entries such as, 'When Odo received it it was worth ten shillings now it is worth thirty shillings.'

So the ownership of land became the mark of the warrior elite. Without land you did not have the cash to finance a decent fighting retinue, and without a fighting retinue you were a man of little account. As the middle ages advanced and as armour improved and became more expensive, so more land was needed to provide the income to pay for the equipment necessary to put a knight in the field.

The concept of the landowner being part of the warrior elite obtains throughout our history, and even today a casual flick through the pages of *Debrett* will show that a far larger percentage of landowners than of any other category of people serve some time in the armed forces, and are proud of it. Old habits and traditions die hard and the concept of serving one's country in return for owning land is still amazingly alive and well. The armed forces aside, landowners continue to spend an inordinate amount of unpaid time serving on local committees of worthy causes and on bodies such as the Country Landowners Association (CLA). I have often wondered what would happen to country life if suddenly landowners demanded to be paid for the vast amount of work they do free.

Now there are very few 'big houses' which antedate the Tudor period and for this there is a variety of reasons; mainly it is because most of those which did exist prior to 1500 were castles and Cromwell blew the majority of them up during the Civil War.

The medieval equivalent of our eighteenth-century squire lived in a small manor house whose most important room was a large hall which he shared with his retainers, dogs, wife and children. The hall, in other words, was the equivalent of the large family kitchen where today's squire lurks, warming himself beside the Aga, feeding his dogs scraps from his table and finding his peace constantly interrupted by a stream of visitors and children, much no doubt as his medieval forebear did.

Unlike his modern descendant however our medieval squire's estate was unlikely all to be located around one central manor house. Instead his land was probably scattered in various sized chunks over several counties; he would thus have been forced to spend an inordinate amount of time on the road travelling between parts of his far-flung empire, setting up his home in a different manor house every few months. There was, therefore, little incentive for him to build a large edifice on any one part of his estate when he was obliged to be absent so much of the time.

The frequency of civil war and rebellion must also have weighed against any lavish building enterprise. It would, to say the least, have been decidedly tedious to have spent rather more than one could afford on erecting a grand house, only to have it burnt down by the revolting peasants or by one's next door neighbour, who, just happening to be on the opposite side, fancied a bit of rape and pillage with his chums after a particularly good dinner. Politics was considerably more fun in those days – though it has to be said the penalties for getting it wrong were rather more severe.

So the chances are your 'big house' will not be much older

than the 1540s, built on the back of some astute financial dealings in the days of bluff King Hal, probably by a *nouveau riche* courtier with his greasy hands firmly in the till. It was the dissolution of the monasteries in 1536, possibly the first historical 'privatisation' ever carried out, which provided such a boost to the country house. Suddenly about a quarter of the acreage of England was up for grabs, and grabbed it was in no uncertain way. Some of it was given in large chunks by the king to deserving courtiers and civil servants but the vast majority was sold off on the open market at knock-down prices. Sounds more and more like a modern privatisation, doesn't it? Anyway, it provided a unique opportunity for many landowners to buy big blocks of land marching with one of their estates. This chance they seized with alacrity, often paying for it by selling outlying land to other buyers. Thus the dissolution of the monasteries caused a major restructuring of the pattern of land ownership throughout England.

Those who accumulated land at this time quickly found that they had made astute purchases. The population of Tudor England was growing, and agriculture, by the latter part of the sixteenth century, was booming. It is perhaps an obvious point, but one sometimes overlooked, that, on the whole, the periods of great country-house building and improvements mirror those of agricultural prosperity.

So with rents rising and estates restructured the stage was set for the advent of that peculiar invention of the English – the country house. One other factor only was needed to prime a building boom – peace and political stability. This the Tudors – after a fashion – provided.

Once the idea had caught on, it took off with a vengeance, and England must have reverberated to the sound of the hammer and saw. The most spectacular houses where those constructed by the parvenu men of business recruited by the Tudor monarchs to manage their affairs in the place of the old aristocracy, whose numbers had been sadly depleted by the blood bath of the Wars of the Roses. Families like the Thynnes of Longleat, the Cecils of Burghley and Hatfield, and the Cavendishes at Hardwick and Bolsover Castle erected great mansions (which the architectural historian, John Summerson, nicknamed 'prodigy houses') to advertise to all that they had now arrived. One suspects that the local gentry, viewing these edifices, sniggered among themselves at their vulgarity and scoffed at the 'modern' conveniences – much as we do today when we hear that some multi-millionaire has spent tens of thousands of pounds on installing sunken baths in his house. It is one of the great jokes of history that every generation regards the buildings of the previous one as in the worst possible taste. Indeed the only reason why so many old houses survive at all is because the original builders frequently nearly bankrupted themselves constructing an over-grand house, so removing the wherewithal from their heirs to knock it down and start again. This rule did not, of course, apply to the mega-rich families, like the Grosvenors, Dukes of Westminster, who, as the Duke of Bedford dryly wrote in 1960, after seeing the plans for a new country house to replace the Victorian Eaton Hall: 'It seems to me that one of the virtues of the Grosvenor family is that they frequently demolish their stately home. I trust future generations will continue the tradition.'

The desire of those grown rich in trade or public office to buy an estate and build a country house is one of the themes which runs throughout the history of the development of the country house and estate; another is the English aristocrats' love of the country. As early as the fifteenth century an Italian observer, Poggio Bracciolini, reported:

> The English think it ignominious for noblemen to stay in the cities. They live in the country, cut off by woods and fields. They devote themselves to country pursuits, selling wood and cattle, and they think it no shame to make money from agriculture. I have seen a man who has given up trade, bought an expensive estate, and left town to go there with his family, turn his sons into noblemen, and himself be accepted by the noble class.

Defoe, writing at the beginning of the eighteenth century, noted how 'the present increase of wealth in the City of London spreads itself into the country, and plants families and fortunes, who in another age will equal the families of the ancient gentry, who perhaps where bought out.' An observation which, come to think about it, could have been made in the mid-1990s.

There was a pause in country-house building during the reign of Charles I and the Commonwealth for obvious reasons and inevitably a boom when Charles II came to the throne in 1660. But this time very different houses were constructed for many of those busy building had spent years in exile on the continent and had seen what the Dutch and French were up to and wanted to replicate the style in England's green and pleasant land.

Connoisseurs consider the period 1660–1730 to have produced many of the most beautiful country houses. It saw a unique flowering in architecture which produced such giants as Hawksmoor, Vanbrugh, Wren, Archer and Talman in England and Bruce in Scotland, among many others. Houses where built which today are still eminently liveable in and had not yet reached the stage of pomposity and pretension which later architects, followers of Palladio, achieved for their clients.

Much has been made of the love of the countryside and of his estates which caused the English nobleman and squire to devote so much time and money to his home in the country. There is some justification for this, but it is also fair to say that the size of the English country house grew, in the eighteenth century, in direct proportion to the power of Parliament. As Parliament became more powerful, at the expense of the Crown, so the ability to ensure your man was elected to one of the local seats became more important. The electorate being strictly limited in those far-off days, it was possible for a nobleman to help his cause by being able to entertain lavishly and impress the electorate with his grandiose mansion and park. The whole became a virtual circle. If the aim of having a number of MPs in your pocket was achieved then ministerial office would probably follow with all the many opportunities attendant upon it for filling your coffers; you would then spend your ill-gotten gains on further embellishments to your pile. Sir Robert Walpole's grand house at Houghton is the quintessential example of how the system could be made to work.

Such was the growth in the building of large houses that it is hardly surprising that the authorities sought ways of taxing such naked display of wealth and success. This had been tried before, back in Tudor times, when a hearth tax had been introduced; not unnaturally this had proved unpopular and had the added disadvantage that the tax assessor had to gain entry to the property to count the hearths. So in 1697 it was replaced by a new stratagem, the window tax. Like many ideas this looked (on paper) a good one – easy to assess and virtually impossible to avoid – until, that is, mean bastards like my ancestors blocked up sixty per cent of their windows! The tax was finally abolished in 1851, but it was not until 1992 that I finished opening up all those windows – such are the long-term effects of stupid taxation policies.

When we admire the glories of the country houses, it certainly does not do to examine too closely the means which enabled them to be built. Our ancestors were as grasping and immoral in their business dealings as the worst type of modern financial fraudster. Robert Maxwell would have been very much at home in eighteenth-century England and two hundred and fifty years later we would, in all likelihood, be wandering round his house, after paying our fiver, admiring his good taste and pictures and perhaps subscribing some of our hard-earned cash to a fund launched by English Heritage to 'save' for the nation a picture painted by an Italian for an Italian which via some shady dealer has metamorphosed into a important part of the British national heritage.

The various reform acts of the mid-nineteenth century destroyed much of the political power of the gentry and nobility but by then the aristocracy was so deeply in thrall to the romance of the country house that the building craze hardly faltered; indeed, it was to receive new impetus from the Industrial Revolution.

The Industrial Revolution provided the engine house for estates in two ways. First, the rapidly expanding urban population had to be fed, and in spite of the repeal of the Corn Laws in 1846 the price of wheat and food remained high, on the whole, right up to the start of the great agricultural depression in 1873. At the same time, many landowners found to their delight that they had coal under their land or a port from which it could be exported, and consequential riches in the form of royalties flooded into their bank accounts.

Meanwhile a new class of people were beginning to cast envious eyes at what they saw as the beau ideal presented by an English country gentleman's existence. Industrialists, mill-owners, shopkeepers and the like were making serious money and the one thing they desired more than anything else, like their predecessors throughout history, was to become gentry. To achieve this aim they were willing to spend any amount on buying an estate and erecting a grandiose house on it in the latest fashion. This they did, and as the nineteenth century progressed the houses became bigger and grander – not this time because a large house might bring them political influence but because, with the advent of the railways, the era of the house party had arrived, coinciding neatly with the surge in popularity of driven-game shooting.

If towards the end of the nineteenth century the traditional landowner with his agricultural estate was feeling a chill wind blowing from across the North Atlantic as British markets were flooded with cheap food, causing his rents to fall, our industrialist friends where wallowing in cash and finding that effectively, providing they could lay on a good shoot and lavish entertainment, they could buy themselves into the first circles socially. Once again, I suspect that the old aristocracy sniggered at the parvenus in their neo-Jacobean mansions – but no one turns down a good day's shooting. You may by now begin to see the purpose of casting a quick eye over history, it has a uncanny habit of repeating itself. After all, most of those doing the sniggering where descended from the Tudor or Georgian *nouveaux riches* themselves!

It was, of course, not only in England that the new rich spent money. Queen Victoria had made the Highlands of Scotland fashionable and there were many impoverished Scottish landowners with hundreds of thousands of acres of barren hillside which they could be persuaded to part with. Scotland had one other great advantage – a unique architectural style, Scottish Baronial, tailor-made for your rich industrialist who had read the works of Sir Walter Scott and who was of a romantic frame of mind. The love affair with Scottish sporting estates started by Queen Victoria still continues today, and many rich Europeans as well as Englishmen are to be found who are willing to buy thousands of acres of barren scrub and happily spend hundreds of thousands of pounds, if not millions, on their new-found romantic dreamworld – owning a Scottish sporting estate having, not inaccurately, been described as the equivalent of tearing up ten-pound notes all day under a cold shower.

The houses these nineteenth-century plutocrats built had to be massive, for the late Victorian and Edwardian era was the high point for domestic servants. In 1900 domestic service was the single biggest source of employment in the UK, with over two and a half million people in the industry. Houses had to be big enough to accommodate not only the small army of servants who lived there but also to allow for the fact that people who came to stay tended to bring their own maids and valets.

Meanwhile as the *nouveaux riches* made hay the traditional land-owning squirearchy and nobility were beginning to feel the pressure of falling incomes and rising taxation. The year 1873 marked the start of a disastrous hundred-year decline in the fortunes of the landed classes. The agricultural depression alone they could no doubt have handled, but gradually they were to be assailed by punitive increases in taxation. Death duties where introduced in 1894 and as the twentieth century progressed, income tax was to rise to confiscatory levels. At the same time the real wages of workers rose inexorably, and during World War I legislation aimed at controlling rents on houses and agricultural land was introduced.

Now we have arrived at the present day, but before we start looking at modern country estates and houses we ought first to consider what is a country estate in contemporary terms? After all it might be a small red-brick house in the Home Counties with twenty-five acres of land which, when put in the hands of an estate agent and advertised for sale, metamorphoses into 'a desirable small self-contained estate situated in the unspoilt countryside of rural Surrey'. This I am afraid is no more an estate than 'a property situated in a select development on an exclusive estate'. (Incidentally, the one thing anyone who is anybody wants to run a mile from is something called 'an exclusive estate'; the only thing likely to be 'select' about the development is the amount you are going to be overcharged for living there.) No, an estate in our context means a large country house with a park and a thousand acres or so of farmland and woods, plus a few cottages.

Of course, one cannot be too doctrinaire about this definition. Many would argue that an estate can be much smaller than this, but I would draw the line at anything much less than a thousand acres as the income is likely to be so paltry that you are going to have to go out and work elsewhere and then how can you be a country gentleman? Strangely this definition fits the parameters of a manor established by William the Conqueror over nine hundred years ago! Not that a thousand acres of land is going to produce enough income for most people to grow fat on, but it might just enable you to live the life of a rather poor country gentleman.

Oh dear, we are already on the subject of money, but then being a country gentleman and keeping up an estate is – at the end of day – about money, so I am afraid the subject will crop up with monotonous regularity throughout the rest of this book. Someone once said – probably that arch-charlatan Sigmund Freud – that a man thinks of sex at least once every five minutes; well, I am not sure about that, but I do know a country gentleman thinks of money every five minutes. If a romantic observer assumes that the last thing an English country gentleman talks or thinks about is money, then he is mistaken. In truth he thinks and talks about little else and, if he didn't, the family pile would soon find its way into the pages of *Country Life*.

A thousand acres may be the minimum size for an estate, but there is no upper limit, nor is there such a thing as a typical estate. It is estimated that there are only some twelve hundred estates left in the United Kingdom and although these range in size from enormous Scottish fiefdoms of a hundred thousand acres of little more than heather, to highly valuable English agricultural estates of twenty thousand acres plus, the majority of estates range between one thousand and five thousand acres.

Just as estates vary in size so they vary in every aspect of their make-up, but perhaps they fall into two distinct categories: those which are lavishly maintained and are, ostensibly, well-managed thriving entrepreneurial establishments, and those which appear to be anything but. The first classification will have an immaculately done-up house, smooth tarmacked drives and gleaming farm machinery in the home farm. The second category will have rough drives, peeling paint and worn carpets within the house and probably does not bother with an in-hand farm at all. Strangely it is often the 'immaculate' estates which end up in the pages of *Country Life*, while the knackered numbers muddle through and survive.

Having defined what an estate is the next thing to do is to break it down into its constituent parts. These are often called, in estate parlance, 'departments'. A landowner may be heard to say rather grandly that he is meeting tomorrow with the head of his 'woodland department', which will impress nearly everyone except those other landowners present who will smile wryly and mentally subtract a notional twenty-five thousand off their friend's net income. For it is a sad fact that few departments seem to make any money; why this is we will examine later.

But back to salient features of our estate. There is, of course, the big house, then come the shooting or game department, the woods, the home farm, tenanted farms, cottages and perhaps a garden. Involved with each of these departments there will be people who fall into two categories full- or part-time employees and outside professionals – consultants, land agents, accountants and the like. We will be looking at all these people and their roles in later chapters, so don't worry.

CHAPTER 2

The Big House

Hail! to thy pile! More honour'd in thy fall
  Than modern mansions in their pillar'd state,
Proudly defiant frowns thy vaulted hall,
  Scowling defiance on the blasts of fate.

BYRON, Elegy on Newstead Abbey

So much for the past. What of the present? Let us begin by looking at what for most people is the central and most visible feature of an estate, the Big House. It goes without saying, having skimmed through, in the preceding chapter, the historical background to the building of these piles, that most stately-home owners are today saddled with houses several times too big for their everyday needs. Gone is the requirement to entertain Queen Elizabeth on one of her progresses through her realm. No longer, sadly, can we hope to bribe and impress a small electorate into returning our choice as member for the county. As for the armies of servants, they have almost totally disappeared.

Hardly surprising then that over the last eighty years or so a great many owners have bitten the bullet and had their houses demolished or arranged for them to be accidentally burnt down – a more sensible solution altogether as not only did the owner get rid of a monstrous liability but he also picked up a bonus in the form of an insurance pay-out. Many owners right up to the early 1980s would, I suspect, have subscribed to the thoughts of the fictional Sir Murgatroyd Sprockett-Sprockett in P. G. Woodhouse's book *Young Men* (1922): 'Here we are and here we have got to stay, mouldering on in this blasted barracks of a place which eats up every penny of my income . . . ', and given joyful thanks for an opportune fire.

The roll-call of casualties was graphically illustrated by the exhibition in 1975 at the Victoria & Albert Museum entitled 'The Destruction of the Country House'. It estimated that some eleven hundred houses in England, Scotland and Wales had been either demolished, burnt or substantially altered since 1900, of which four hundred and twenty-three where demolished or burnt between 1922 and 1955.

A grievous loss – especially if you agree with the view of the architectural historian John Harris that, 'The unity of a great house with its furnished interior, collection of great pictures and sculpture, its library and family and estate archives, tied within a garden and set in a landscaped park, is perhaps the supreme example of a collective work of art.'

But the purpose of the exhibition was not just to catalogue past losses but to focus attention on the threat to those remaining houses still in private hands. It is easy to forget just how grim things looked only twenty-three years ago. There was a newly elected Labour government whose chancellor, Denis Healey, had announced his intention of squeezing the rich 'till the pips squeaked', and to that end was intending to introduce a wealth tax on top of the reforms to death duties aimed at making them virtually unavoidable.

At the time it looked as if communism, masquerading as socialism, had triumphed, and that the long delayed death of the English landed estate was finally at hand. Few, if any, saw that this was the last gasp of a discredited economic and social dogma or recognised in the new leader of the Conservative opposition, Margaret Thatcher, the heroic figure who, almost single-handed, would have the guts, five years later, to take on the task of rolling back some fifty years of socialism. For if there is one person who has done more than any other, over the last hundred years, to stop the disintegration of the remaining great estates, it is Margaret Thatcher, the daughter of a shopkeeper.

But the list of destruction catalogued at the V&A is only half the story. The other half concerns the many houses which, in a sense, have suffered an even more ignominious fate in being converted for various forms of institutional use – either as schools, training colleges, hotels or company headquarters – or carved up into flats. At a guess I would think this has been the

fate of at least a further thousand houses. It is true that
occasionally a house returns from institutional use to private
hands. My favourite example is that of the current Lord
Portsmouth's ancestral home, Farley House. It had been let as a
prep school to which as a boy he was sent. He so hated the
school, and most of the masters, that he vowed if he was ever in
a position to do so, he would send them packing. Years later the
lease came to an end and, much to the surprise of the school, it
was not renewed.

So from a figure (admittedly debatable) of approximately five
thousand country houses and estates in private hands at the turn
of the century we are now down to around twelve hundred, a
reduction of some seventy-five per cent. I say the figure of five
thousand is debatable because no clear definition exists of what
constitutes a country house and estate, thus no comprehensive
catalogue exists either. However, various people have tackled
this subject using a variety of sources, such as the 'Index to the
Principal Seats in the United Kingdom' contained in Walford's
County Families of the United Kingdom, which lists 3,321 such
places in England and a further 1,974 in Scotland, Wales and
Ireland, and Bateman's *The Great Landowners of Great Britain
and Ireland*, which lists, in 1873, 1,323 estates in England with
more than three thousand acres and a further 617 estates with
between two and three thousand acres. Hence a total of five
thousand existing in the United Kingdom around 1900 looks
about right.

The first man to warn the general public of the approaching
Armageddon was Lord Lothian who, in a keynote address to the
then tiny National Trust in 1934, warned of an impending crisis;
the country house, he said, was doomed:

> Most of these [country houses] are now under sentence of
> death, and the axe which is destroying them is taxation, and
> especially that form of taxation known as death duties . . . I
> don't think it is an exaggeration that within a generation
> hardly one of these historic houses will be lived in by the
> families who created them. Yet it is these four or five
> hundred families who have guided the future of this nation.

That speech set in train the National Trust's country-house programme which 'saved' over one hundred houses between 1950 and 1960.

I suppose the time has come to address the problem of why so many owners threw in the towel. There are, of course, many reasons, mainly financial, but the one which no one really touches on is the most important – defeat. From 1873 onwards landowners had been under almost continuous attack from increases in taxation, falling agricultural incomes and enormous inflation in wages, at a time when most of their incomes were static or falling. They then had to suffer the impact of two World Wars.

The Second World War may have been, in some ways, the finest hour of the country house, but it was also to prove the death of many as a consequence of their role in the war; houses built and maintained for the pleasure of their occupants or to impress the neighbouring gentry were converted into army headquarters, training camps, officers' messes and the like. Over two thousand houses were requisitioned for use by the armed forces and when in 1945 their owners returned from the fighting to take back their ancestral properties they found, more often than not, that they had been barbarously treated. The compensation offered by the government to put right the damage was, in most cases, derisory. John Harris, in his book, *No Voice from the Hall,* tells the story of Roll Park, in Essex – a by no means untypical example. It was requisitioned by the army in 1939 and when Andrew Lloyd (the owner) returned from the war

> he discovered that no less that eighteen different regiments had occupied the house; they had hacked up the delectable Tudor back staircase for firewood, and had begun on the Grinling Gibbons front staircase. In the saloon Allan Ramsay's famous portrait of Emma Harvey had been used as a dart board and she had been endowed with a moustache . . . the conservative estimate given to Lloyd for repairs was £50,000, a huge sum then; the government offered £8,000. As he wrote to me: 'I threw in my hand in 1943 and allowed the house too be demolished. It was all too much.'

Low levels of compensation were only part of the problem; in post-war Britain draconian building regulations severely limited the supply of materials, so even those owners who had both the will and the cash to restore their properties were often unable to do anything about it.

One hammer blow after another had hit them and none of them could imagine in their most optimistic moments that their heir would ever want to live in the house anyway or, even if he did, would have the income necessary to keep it up. But they were sometimes mistaken. The case of Sir Francis Dashwood is by no means unique. He was on exercise with his regiment in Germany when he received a telegram from his father: 'Hurray! The National Trust have agreed to take on the house.' Sir Francis was furious but there was nothing he could do – the deed had been done.

It is easy to forget how appalling the future looked then to country-house owners. A flavour of the despair felt by many can be gained from reading the late James Lees-Milne's riveting diaries of his travels round England and Wales, on behalf of the National Trust, during and after the war. This extract on Lyme Park is typical:

> Lord Newton is hopeless. The world is too much for him, and no wonder, he does not know what he can do, ought to do, or wants to do. He just throws up his hands in despair. The only thing he is sure about is that his descendants will never want to live at Lyme, after an unbroken residence of six hundred years . . . Lady Newton is as languid and hopeless as her husband. Both said they would never be able to reconcile themselves to the new order after the war. They admitted that their day was done, and life as they had known it was gone for ever. How right they are, poor people.

And this air of defeatism remained a major factor for many years after the war. As recently as 1973, James Lees-Milne predicted that: 'The English House is an archaic osprey. The few left fulfilling the purpose for which they were built are inexorably doomed.' Ironically, since those words where written, both the osprey and the country house have taken on a new lease of life.

Consider these words spoken in Parliament on the subject of taxing houses and landowners:

> They employ hundreds of people and labourers of every description, and they give amusement and enjoyment to thousands. In the summer months the means of conveying the people who go to see these places becomes an absolute industry in itself. But if properties like these, which are blessed or encumbered with a Chatsworth, are to be mulcted in the manner which you propose, the inevitable consequence will be that one after the other they will be shut up, their contents will be sold and dispersed, the whole army of people to whom they give occupation throughout the year will be dismissed and their employment gone, and money will no longer be attracted to the neighbourhood.

Prophetic words indeed – now guess when they where spoken. In 1894, during the debate on Sir William Harcourt's finance bill which brought in death duties! Henry Chaplin was the MP who spoke them.

Incidentally, in a nice touch of irony, the heiress of the 2nd Viscount Harcourt, and direct descendant of Sir William, was hit by massive death duties on the death of her father. David Littlejohn, in his book *The Fate of the English Country House* (1997), chronicles the misery which these taxes caused the Honourable Mrs Gasgoine. She told him:

> There was no possible way we could pay the death duties when my father died in 1979, so we reluctantly agreed to permit public access. It is very upsetting and frustrating – every item exempt from taxes must be kept available for the public to see! They tell you how many days you have to open, where you have to advertise. They simply ignore the fact that a house this size is *lived* in – there's nowhere for the family to withdraw.

My sympathy for her plight is considerably reduced when I recall the misery and impoverishment her ancestor's policy has wrought on so many other families. A quote from Horace seems apt : 'Undeservedly you will atone for the sins of your fathers.'

Perhaps Mrs Gascoigne should have it carved in stone above her front door?

But back to the doom-mongers. This quote is from *Rural Estate Management* by Charles Walmsley in 1948: 'The large country house with its surrounding estate is doomed by death duties and taxation.' This extract is from the Historic Buildings Council's report in 1954: 'It is unlikely that many of the large historic houses, even those at present in a good state of repair, will remain much longer in private ownership, maintained entirely at the owner's expense.' Lawrence Stone, in his book *An Open Elite,* published in 1986, wrote: 'The alternatives of survival are manifold, but the efforts seemed doomed.' In short the obituary of the country house has been written ceaselessly for almost a hundred years, yet strangely the patient has refused to die. Why?

There is really only one reason why there are still some twelve hundred country houses with estates left in the United Kingdom today – pure bloody-minded determination on the part of the owners; that old-fashioned word 'guts' springs to mind, something most inhabitants of this country are now sadly lacking as they go squealing to lawyers or MPs with the slightest grievance, real or imagined. For the best part of a hundred years these families have held on grimly to their inheritance as the various governments of the day have done their level best to force them to sell and demolish their houses; now they find to their surprise and amazement that their properties are part of the 'National Heritage'.

It is a peculiar thing this National Heritage; 'the nation' decrees that a building is part of its 'heritage', but in spite of this, as we shall see, makes no contribution to the costs of maintaining it – in fact, it taxes those who do maintain it! Odd. Even odder though is the concept that something should belong to the nation when the nation has not spent one penny on building it or buying the items it contains. Strange, I think, you will agree. Personally I do not believe my house is anything to do with the National Heritage as the only time the nation took any particular interest in it was when Cromwell's cannons tried to knock holes in it during the Civil War. But then the devaluation of words and the changing of their meaning are characteristic of the times we live in.

But let us look more closely at the country house today and at how the modern owner can ensure its survival for his own posterity.

Whatever the date or size of your house certain things will be common to all. It will of course be BIG. There are small country houses, of course, little gems of the Queen Anne era, for instance, with a few acres of land, but we are not concerned with them. How big is BIG? People often ask how many rooms a house has, forgetting that the number is frankly irrelevant. A decent sized great hall or state drawing room may, quite possibly, be large enough to swallow an entire detached five-bedroom executive home! In other words, the number of rooms is no indication of a house's size.

A better measure is to take the square footage of the floor plan, but even this is fallible as many of the grander rooms will soar the entire height of a house. However, a line must be drawn somewhere, so let us draw it at twelve thousand square feet, which would be the area covered by a reasonably spacious family-sized house, albeit relatively modest compared to many houses.

So we have our big house. It will come with the normal mixture of large state rooms, family quarters and attic accommodation, as well as kitchens, larders, pantries and the like, designed for when the house was run by a small army of servants. If your house is Victorian or Edwardian the area devoted to the space behind the green-baize door is likely to be vast and a continuing headache (unless you were fortunate and your father demolished it).

So what do you do with this rambling barracks? Well the simple answer is, live in it and enjoy it. Big houses are marvellous in many ways. You can, for instance, take a walk inside when its raining, your children can ride their bicycles around the corridors and rooms and play endless games. A lot of fun can be had by all the family in exploring and looking through old chests in derelict rooms in the hope of finding something valuable to sell at Christies. In short big houses should not be taken too seriously.

Sadly that is what people do now – take their big house seriously. They worry about the maintenance, about the running costs, they worry about the damage the children are doing when using the Elizabethan bed hangings as climbing ropes. Life, in fact, ceases to be any fun at all.

A lot of this worry is caused by the 'cult of the country house' which over the last twenty-odd years has grown enormously – ever since, in fact, that V&A exhibition which predicted the eventual demise of the whole shooting match. There is a lot to worry about, too, if you are that way inclined and actually bother to take what the so-called experts say seriously. A few years ago, I bought a book entitled *The National Trust Book on House-keeping.* In my innocence, I thought it might contain helpful hints on how to look after my things. Not a bit of it; every time it got on to something interesting the paragraph ended with the depressing advice to 'consult an expert'. It was rather like reading a Joan Collins book with all the sex scenes cut out.

Experts incidentally are the bane of a country-house owner's life. Strangely they all have one distinguishing feature – none of them have ever lived in a big house. They ponce round one's home, shaking their silken locks dolefully at the peeling wall-paper and the decrepit paintwork, look learnedly at the bulging masonry and crumbling rendering and pronounce that the bill to put it all right will run into millions. Relax – they are ignorant gits who know nothing; your house will stand for many years with a minimum of maintenance, providing you keep the water out.

The real trouble with most of these so-called 'experts' is that they haven't a clue what they are talking about. They rave over the ghastly chair-covers great-aunt Agatha installed and ask you what you doing to 'preserve' them! Then are horrified to learn that the only reason why they have not been consigned to the bonfire years ago is that you have not got enough money to replace them. They admire the fact you seem to live in a time warp, forgetting that it is financial necessity, not choice, which stops you ripping down walls, painting ceilings, hanging new curtains and re-covering the chairs. They forget also that what they admire today is the result of several hundred years of past generations behaving in exactly that way.

All this, I suppose, neatly brings us on to the subject of listed buildings, English Heritage and its Scottish and Welsh equivalents. Virtually every pile is 'listed' and most are either Grade 1 or Grade 2*. Now, quite often, ignorant people take pride in the fact that their house is listed – at which one raises one's eyes to the ceiling and sighs. English Heritage has actually had the nerve to state that listing increases the value of a building. This, of course, is rubbish, and anyway, even if it were true, it is totally irrelevant from the point of view of owners who have no intention of selling. No, the reason the value of listed buildings is high is they happen to be, by definition, rather beautiful buildings; it has nothing to do with whether they are listed or not. Listing though, for those who don't know, is one of those pernicious forms of covert nationalisation without compensation which have, like a cloud of poisonous gas on a damp morning on the Somme in 1916, been slowly creeping over the countryside, destroying and sterilising everything in their path.

The aim of course is laudable – to stop unscrupulous people destroying the architectural heritage of this country; and when one looks at what the local authorities, planners, and developers have managed to achieve since the war one has to agree that some such legislation was necessary. But here is the irony – guess who is in charge of giving consent to planning applications on listed buildings? Why the local authorities, of course! Yes, the very same ones who have succeeded so ably in ruining most of our historic towns.

The origins of the listing process go back to 1943 when the then Ministry of Town and Country Planning drew up a national inventory of historic buildings. Come 1947, with a Labour government firmly in the saddle, an act was brought in to control the alteration and demolition of listed buildings and, if necessary, to allow for their compulsory purchase.

It is, of course, one thing to pass an Act of Parliament and quite another to make it effective. Even 'mentally challenged' individuals, such as the then chancellor Hugh Dalton, began to realise that with taxation at stratospheric levels (he had recently raised death duties to seventy-five per cent) owners of many listed buildings simply did not have the cash to maintain them. Now, some writers hold that Hugh Dalton is the great saviour of the English Country House as, in his 1948 budget, he invented something called the Land Fund. This was to consist of some fifty million pounds raised by the sale of War Surplus. The intention was that it would be used to buy important houses, land and works of art for 'the nation'. As the only reason that the owners where having to sell them was that 'the nation' was taxing them at such a high level, what he was actually proposing was a sort of Alice in Wonderland situation in which the nation bought land and buildings from owners who had to sell them to pay the taxes which the government needed to pay for the land and buildings.

Anyway he introduced this wizard scheme in his famous budget broadcast to the nation saying that: 'I want to help the Ramblers' Association, the Youth Hostel Association and the National Trust in the fine work they are doing.'

The sudden concern of Hugh Dalton and his successor as chancellor, Sir Stafford Cripps, for the future of historic houses was strange, but even stranger is the rapturous applause which their acts are today accorded. Some even credit them with 'saving' the stately homes. I find this perplexing. It was rather as if someone who had been doing his best to drown you, suddenly, just as you were about to snuff it, let go of your head and allowed you to come up for air. Had he 'saved' your life? Well only in the sense that he had nearly killed you in the first place and then relented.

Be that as it may, Cripps it was who set up the Gower Committee to report on the future of the historic house. It was published in 1950 and is worth quoting from:

> In past times great houses . . . were maintained by their owners . . . now we are faced with a disaster comparable only to that suffered at the dissolution of the monasteries . . . Taxation is primarily responsible for this impending cata- strophe. The present rates mean that no individual, however

much his gross income, or whatever its source, can have much more than £5,000 to spend. Only seventy taxpayers in the country are left with more than £6,000 a year; and that sum represents a gross income of about £100,000. Many great houses need not less than £5,000 a year, some as much as £10,000 a year, to maintain them, not to any luxury standard, but to the minimum necessary to preserve them and their contents from deterioration . . . Particulars were given us of one case in which a gross income of £140,000 is reduced to £3,500 after income tax, tithe, surtax and expenses of maintaining the agricultural estate from which it comes. Out of this the owner has to maintain two historic houses, as well as himself and his family. He can only do this by drawing on capital at the rate of £8,000 a year.

Every estate owner should read this report if only to help him understand the appalling situation his father or grandfather was faced with at that time. No wonder so many sold their land and demolished their houses; the wonder is that so many did not!

The Gower Report made many radical recommendations, many of which were acted upon, and virtually all legislation regarding stately homes and listed buildings can be traced back to this document. However, in spite of the legislation, the unchanging tax regime meant that houses continued to disappear. Between 1950 and 1975 a further two hundred and fifty where to be demolished.

One of the primary reasons for the continuing saga was that like much legislation designed to safeguard something for the public good the public was, and is, not prepared to pay for it. As recently as 1995, Stephen Dorrell, then Secretary of State for Heritage, said: 'The principal responsibility for caring for listed buildings rests with the owners. But others have an interest.' Quite so. But when I have an interest I normally expect to pay for it, not to make a thumping great profit.

Let me explain. There are some 440,000 listed buildings in England and Wales of which 6,067 are Grade 1 and around 17,250 Grade 2*, the remainder being Grade 2.

Now, let us, for amusement's sake, do some basic arithmetic, concentrating on the Grade 1 and Grade 2* buildings where the planning requirements are most stringent. Assume for the sake of argument that on average each one of these 23,300 buildings requires a minimum average of £10,000 spent per annum on essential maintenance and building work. The total amount spent annually therefore comes to £230,300,000 – chunky money you will agree. Now we have already seen that the public considers it important that these buildings are kept up to an acceptable standard and indeed owners are forced by law to make sure this is done. But what financial help does the taxpayer give? None. Instead it takes 17.5% of the total spent on essential repairs as tax. So the taxman's 'profit' on listed buildings is running at approximately £40,330,000 per annum. Of course, if I grease enough palms and get planning permission in a unspoilt village to build an excrescence of a bungalow, complete with a Marley tile roof and PVC windows, plus a fake modern Georgian front door, then no VAT will be charged. Somehow it doesn't seem quite right.

There is of course a simple solution – make repairs to listed buildings exempt from VAT – but successive governments have resisted this. The main excuse is that any changes to VAT have to be approved by the relevant European commissioner, but I suspect that they also think that if repairs were VAT exempt, an awful lot of unimportant building work, such as painting and decorating, installing a new Jacuzzi in a bathroom, etc., would be put down as 'essential repairs'. It is an argument that I have some sympathy with. The counter is that only approved repairs should be non-vatable, but then that would cause an explosion of bureaucracy – something everyone is very keen to avoid.

Is there a solution? Yes, I think there is, and one which would have all the advantages of being cheap and easy to administer and for which one would not need the hated European Union's permission. It is called Depreciation. This is a trick well known to accountants and businessmen. In short, if you buy a machine with a working life of ten years you are allowed to depreciate the cost of the machine over its anticipated lifetime and set the annual amount of its depreciation against your profits for tax purposes.

My idea, which I offer free to the Heritage Secretary, is that listed buildings should be allowed to depreciate the anticipated cost of their repairs as per a simple formula. Those of us who live in these buildings know that the lifespan of most repairs is between fifty and a hundred years. A slate roof, for instance, should last the full hundred and lead slightly longer, but electric wiring needs doing every thirty-odd years otherwise the chances are the entire house will go up in smoke – and so on.

The concept is this. That the square footage of every listed building is measured by a reputable surveyor and a tax allowance is granted to that building on a square-foot basis. So a twenty-thousand-square-foot building might need, at today's prices, something approaching two million pounds spent on essential repairs over a hundred-year period, or a hundred pounds per square foot (unless, that is, it is one owned by the National Trust – but we will be looking at that in more detail later). Each year the owners would be able to set against tax twenty thousand pounds' worth of repairs against tax or, and this is important, roll the tax relief forward for the big job that they know needs doing in ten years' time.

Simple isn't it – relatively foolproof – relatively free of bureaucracy – *ergo* – obviously a non-starter.

Actually, the profit to the treasury on listed buildings is even greater than I have estimated, because the other side of the equation is what it would cost the taxpayer to keep most of these buildings in existence if the private owners gave up the unequal struggle. And presumably, as the government insists they are part of the National Heritage, the taxpayer would have no choice but to pay. One admits, of course, that the taxpayer would be unlikely to want to take on all Grade 1 and Grade 2* properties, but surely no one is going to suggest that he could look quietly on as houses of the quality of Chatsworth, Blenheim and the like where sold and converted for institutional use?

We will get a better idea of what the cost savings involved are when we examine the workings of the National Trust in a later chapter, but we can safely assume that it would be vast – hundreds of millions of pounds a year.

In fact, the threat of stately homes falling into ruin if the current owners were forced to give up and sell has receded in recent years. Estate agents have books full of *nouveaux riches* businessmen and bankers wanting to buy estates and large houses, and not just Englishmen either – Europeans, Arabs, Americans, all seem to want to sink their ill-gotten gains into the bottomless pit of a large house and surrounding estate.

Luckily for estate agents and their clients there is still a steady stream of such properties coming on the market. Hugh Montgomery–Massingberd, in his book *The Disintegration of a Heritage*, reckoned that around twenty great houses, with their accompanying estates, were being sold each year. I don't dispute the figures but I do perhaps wonder if the only reasons are high maintenance costs. In my experience sales occur mainly for five reasons: the heir/owner is a drug addict or a spendthrift or, perhaps, horror of horrors, a combination of the two; the owner has lost a packet in a disastrous business venture; the owner has married a very expensive wife; the estate has been left in such dire straits that it is no longer remotely viable, e.g., the daughters and younger sons have been given too generous legacies; and, finally, the owner has been quietly selling his capital assets for years to finance his lifestyle and now with his income reduced he has only the house and the rump of the estate left to sell.

Actually, there is a sixth category of seller – those who have recently bought a stately home and its land. Estate agents love selling stately homes because not only are they prestigious but the chances are they will be back on the market within ten or, at the very most, twenty-five years. Indeed, one large house in Devon called Whiteway has been sold no less than five times in thirty years! The reason for the inability of most new buyers to put down their roots is simple. By the time they are rich enough to afford their dream their own children are grown up, and when ten, twenty years later they suggest to their eldest son that he might like to take over the estate he is totally uninterested, so back it comes on the market – having in the meantime gobbled up a significant amount of money.

In 1988, Nicholas Ridley said, in a speech to the Historic Houses Association, 'There have to be some opportunities for today's *nouveaux riches* so I am not impressed by the case for the *anciens pauvres*.' To which Lord Shelburne, then president of that august body, replied: 'Potentially there are many hundreds of owners who cannot hold on financially much longer . . . When they admit defeat, beaten by the challenge, will there be queues of *nouveaux riches* to take over where they left off? Of course not. Most successful entrepreneurs have more sense!'

Well, Nicholas Ridley was proved right and Lord Shelburne wrong – as he would soon find out today if he put his house, Bowood, on the market.

The reasons behind the sudden appetite of the *nouveaux riches* for country life are many and varied, and most of them probably haven't changed since that Italian wrote in the fifteenth century: 'I have seen a man, who has given up trade, bought an expensive estate and left town with his family, turn his sons into noblemen.'

However, part of the reason is probably something to do with the 'industrial revolution' which has occurred over the last thirty years in house management. Efficient dishwashers, cooking implements, cleaning devices and the like have revolutionised life below stairs in the big houses and have enabled owners to exist in the height of luxury with what before the war would have been considered a skeleton staff. And it is not only inside the house that the mechanical revolution has wrought its work. In the gardens, ride-on lawnmowers and patent weedkillers have enabled large staffs to be reduced while still achieving almost the same overall effect. In short, big houses no longer need big staffs to keep them up.

A further factor is the improvement in roads and all forms of transport which have put previously inaccessible parts of the United Kingdom within reasonable travelling distance of London. But the main reason is, of course, that we now have a relatively benign tax system which leaves more money in people's pockets, and some choose to spend it on the romantic dream of buying a country house and estate.

The result has been a dramatic inflation of prices for such establishments. Back in 1967, a chartered surveyor, John Taylor, was flicking through *Farmers' Weekly* when he saw an idyllic house in a one-thousand-acre estate; it was called Cricket St Thomas, the asking price was £245,000 and he bought it. Over the next thirty years he developed the estate into a leisure complex and wildlife park and in 1997 put it on the market looking for offers in excess of eight million pounds. It is true that – at the time of writing – he has not sold it for that, there being a world of difference between what one asks and what one sometimes gets, and direct comparisons are further complicated by the fact that John Taylor has developed Cricket St Thomas into a major tourist attraction and business. But, at a guess, even without this addition to the property, it would still fetch, today, around five to six million pounds.

But to get back to the cost of maintaining these rambling piles. I seem to be hearing a sort of muttering from somewhere about grants. Grants? oh, yes – those marvellous things dished out by English Heritage. Whenever any owner of an historic house spends any money on it, the first thing his friends say is, 'You must have got a big grant.' When he has fully recovered from being quietly sick he is forced to explain that the chances of getting a *good* grant from English Heritage is on a par with winning the lottery.

To give you some idea. In 1992, English Heritage proudly disposed of £118,328 in grants to houses belonging to members of the Historic Houses Association. This worked out at an average of £85 for every member of the HHA which, bearing in mind the association includes such mammoth establishments as Blenheim, Longleat, Chatsworth and Castle Howard, is an interesting statistic. Another interesting statistic is that between 1953 and 1973 the old predecessor of English Heritage, the Historic Buildings Council, made total grants to private owners over that period of only £2.5 million, or a paltry average of £125,000 a year! Even if we allow for inflation and multiply these figures by a factor of ten to get somewhere near the modern value of money, it will be seen that rarely has the private owner ever received more than the modern equivalent of one million in any one year since the grant system was set up.

In fairness to English Heritage they do have a problem. They have limited funds available, around a hundred million a year,

and an increasing number of properties wanting them, as every
listed Grade 1 and Grade 2* building is able to apply. As this
includes churches, cathedrals, National Trust houses, houses
owned by institutions, etc., the private owner is squeezed out.
Personally, I would be fascinated to see a table comparing the
amount of grant money given to the National Trust for use on
their properties compared to that received by all private owners
over the last twenty-odd years. My suspicion is that the National
Trust, with only two hundred houses and gardens to manage,
has got a far larger slice of the cake.

English Heritage offer some four hundred and fifty grants a
year but are forced to reject one in two applications. They have
made great efforts within the last couple of years to put their
house in order, to make themselves more 'user friendly', and
they express themselves hurt by the continued cynicism of most
private owners towards their organisation. This cynicism,
however, has been built up over the years and exists for very
good reasons. To understand it let's look at a 'case history'.

The owner of a Grade 1 house decides the time has come to
put the roof right, an essential repair and one that would
certainly qualify for grant aid. His first port of call is likely to be
the local builder, who has years of experience of working on the
property and comes up with a quote to do the work for around
£150,000.

Our hypothetical owner rubs his hands with glee, he has
£75,000 in the bank and, with every expectation of getting a
fifty-per-cent grant from English Heritage, he gets in touch with
them. So far so good and so simple. Now for the problems. Has
he got an architect's opinion? No, he doesn't think he needs one.
Wrong, you must get one if you want a grant – kiss goodbye to a
minimum of £5,000.

Does your financial situation warrant a grant? You don't
know? Or perhaps you were not aware that grants are means
tested. Well, they are. There are two bases for assessing your
financial worthiness for a grant. First the market value. Under
this formula you will get your grant providing the cost of the
repair schedule exceeds the market value of the house. When
this rule was first introduced large country houses, frankly,

were worth very little, so it was of purely academic interest. Since those days property values have shot up and, except in the more inaccessible parts of Britain, it would be hard to find a large house which was technically valued at under £500,000. In other words, you have to be into a pretty substantial essential-repair programme to qualify.

The second basis is an Historic Estate Assessment. This is more complex, as you would expect, so stand by for some serious accountant's bills if you chose this route. To begin with it is only open to houses which have been owned for at least three generations by the same family. To find out if you qualify for a grant English Heritage will look in detail at your last three years' accounts and assess whether you have sufficient surplus of income over expenditure to fund your repair programme out of your own resources or whether you need help.

So now get your accountant to do the work – bang goes another £5,000, or far more if you are stupid enough to employ one based in London (of whom more later). Then – is your builder competent, in English Heritage's eyes, to do the work? Perhaps not, so get other quotes from approved builders and find that instead of the job costing £150,000 it is now likely to cost £250,000. You are, I trust, beginning to understand why grants are such a waste of space.

Here is my advice to anyone who still thinks that grants from English Heritage are a good idea: Don't even think about it! Unless, that is, your restoration programme is so vast and your house so important that you are talking serious money, i.e £500,000 plus. It is like opening Pandora's box – once you've opened it, you can't shut it again.

The real joke, of course, is that, as a grant has to be 'approved', you might, after doing all that work and spending all that extra money, not get the grant anyway! Then you really would be in trouble.

In a worst-case scenario you won't get the grant but the experts from English Heritage will discover some rare aspect of your property which no one previously knew about and force you to forgo the modernising of the old kitchen and preserve the 1880 kitchen range you were about to replace with a modern Aga.

You may now be wondering why, if they are so fraught with obstacles, grants are still in existence? A good question. Not only are they virtually valueless as far the vast majority of house owners are concerned, but their very existence causes confusion in the minds of the general public, the latter being under the totally mistaken impression that many stately homes are only kept upright by enormous injections of taxpayers' money. As we have seen, the opposite is the case. Personally, I believe the Historic Houses Association ought to campaign for the abolition of grants to private owners in exchange for a depreciation charge. This would focus the public's attention on the current state of affairs and the paucity of grant money available for private owners.

A last word on grants from Sir John Smith, chairman of the Landmark Trust: 'Accepting a grant from English Heritage is like marrying for money. In the end you earn it. I am not saying you should never do it, but you should only do it for what the French call an "important sum".'

Now is a good time to look at listing. It is, of course, a pernicious process. If you are in possession of a Grade 1 or Grade 2* property, the restrictions on you are onerous – if you bother to abide by them, that is – because listing extends to all buildings within the curtilage, not just the part of your property which attracted the attention of the inspector in the first place. To quote:

> The ground which is used for the comfortable enjoyment of a house or other building may be regarded in law as within the curtilage of that house or building and thereby as an integral part of the same, although it has not been marked off or enclosed in any way. It is enough that it serves the purpose of the house or building in some necessary or reasonable way.

So technically you require listed-building consent to alter or demolish any structure pre-dating 1948 which is within land which fits the above definition.

This, of course, leads to ludicrous situations. Let us assume that a house is listed Grade 1 because the central block of it is an exceptional Queen Anne house. Sadly for the owners, their ancestors were rolling in the loot in the latter part of the nineteenth century and decided to build on a couple of ghastly wings to house the masses of servants they now needed to look after their good selves and their weekend guests. These wings are no longer required and anyone with a brain would see that their demolition would be enormously beneficial both to the family and to the original Queen Anne house.

But because they are attached to a Grade 1 building they are themselves Grade 1! And to get permission to alter a Grade 1 building is a lengthy and costly process, especially today when every obscure architect and style of architecture has a vocal and well-financed interest group.

But let us move on. Apart from construction work the other aspect is running expenses. These are all those ghastly brown envelopes which arrive with the post just as you are settling down to your breakfast and effectively ruin the best meal of the day. Bills for insurance, electricity, maintenance agreements on servicing the Aga, the boiler, the burglar alarm and so on. They all add up to a considerable sum spent annually, but some of them you can at least reduce to manageable proportions. Electric lights, for instance, only need to be turned on when you are in a room, while the central heating need never be switched on at all except when the temperature slips some way below freezing. The best investment anyone can make in a big house is to have a manual on/off switch in the boiler room and remove the timer clock.

Central heating is in fact more a curse than a godsend. The worst thing about it is that all one's friends have it installed these days. They seem to turn it on automatically – regardless of the weather – in October and only turn it off in April; it must cost them a fortune – as I'm reliably informed it does. When they come to stay with me, instead of remarking on the healthy, bracing atmosphere in the house, they ostentatiously start to shiver and make rather weak jokes. When I suggest there is a simple solution to the problem, which would cost me nothing and would do the British wool industry a lot of good, namely the putting on of a jersey, they look at one as though one were a dangerous lunatic.

There is one very good joke about central heating – it causes dry rot. Dry rot is a nasty fungus which thrives in warm, damp conditions. It is, in fact, not native to this country but arrived here in the nineteenth century from the Himalayas, courtesy of plant collectors. Now, one thing dry rot hates more than anything is cold and drafts, it simply cannot abide them, so I have no problems. But I know of a man who spent a fortune renovating a reasonable-sized Cotswold manor house, and to ensure his comfort put in double glazing, roof insulation and central heating. To his horror, within a very short time the entire building was riddled in the fungus and it cost him a tidy sum to put right.

Apart from central heating there are, of course, many other unnecessary costs. Window cleaning springs to mind. I once read of some peer complaining that it cost him ten thousand a year to keep his windows clean. This struck me as odd. What is the point? The outsides of the windows get washed by the rain while the insides can be left to fester until one can't see out of them anymore, but that is only after thirty or fifty years of saving ten thousand a year!

In short a country-house owner needs to look at his costs very carefully. What he must not do is what all too many try to do – live in the house as though it were a nice cosy five-bedroom house in the Home counties. You can of course do it – but you need to be seriously rich, which sadly most country-house owners aren't.

After the last war, several owners came up with an alternative to just living in their houses – opening them to the public. This was not a new idea. Many houses had opened their doors before; indeed, in the eighteenth and nineteenth centuries it was common practice for those with large houses to allow visitors round.

It was in 1871 that *The Times* made the following comment:

> The British public have much to be thankful for . . . Wherever they go they have, within an easy drive, some great place, with park, gardens, very fine oak trees, natural curiosities, and some fine pictures. A moderate gratuity to the servants will often purchase for them as much pleasure as the noble or

gentle owner has in a year for enormous expenditure. He only
goes down, perhaps to bleed money at every pore, to scold, to
give orders, to entertain, and convert his house into a hotel,
with the privilege of paying all the bills. The public, a
chartered libertine, steps in and enjoys a glimpse of Paradise –
as much as is good for any of us – at the moderate cost of a
shilling a head for a party of five, perhaps . . . A Fifth
Monarchy man of the sternest Communist type used to admit
that there was one good in our gentry – they made the country
picturesque. The truth is England would be naked without
them.

Once again we see that nothing changes. *The Times* could print
virtually the same leader today and find few to quarrel with it. It
is true that towards the end of the nineteenth century many
owners had to rethink their open-door policy, as improvements
in communications allowed thousands to visit where before only
a few hundred had come.

Some owners though, even before the First World War, had
already embarked on the commercialisation of their houses. In
1905, Warwick Castle had forty thousand visitors a year paying
a shilling a head and providing a healthy income to the then Earl
of Warwick. But Warwick was, and remained, a rarity in its
pursuit of profit. For most owners who, after the last war,
embarked on opening their houses, the pursuit of profit through
showing visitors round was a radical and, in some instances, an
exciting new concept. Added impetus to this idea was given
when grants for repairs became available, as grants were usually
conditional on the house being opened to the public.

The leaders in this field were, perhaps inevitably, the
descendants of the once hugely rich and corrupt old Whig
families whose ancestors had built massive piles with their ill-
gotten gains in the sixteenth, seventeenth and eighteenth
centuries. Men such as the Duke of Bedford and the Earl of Bath
entered eagerly into the spirit of the business and, while some of
their fellow peers sniffed at the vulgarity of their antics, on the
whole they made a success of it and achieved the aim of saving
their houses from sale or demolition.

Just because the scheme paid off for owners of some of the premier-division houses did not of course mean that every house could successfully follow down the same path. Unfortunately many owners did not realise this obvious fact, and, as house followed house in the rush to open, many found, after spending tens if not hundreds of thousands on providing 'facilities' for the public, that the said public obstinately refused to be tempted to visit in sufficient numbers to pay the running costs of opening the house to them in the first place – let alone give any return on the capital invested. In short, 'opening your house' did not prove to be the gold mine that had been envisaged – though, come to think of it, most gold mines have an irritating way of promising you great riches, if only you are prepared to cough up some of your precious reserve of capital and invest in them, and then failing dismally.

Of course, not every house opened because the owner wanted it to. In many instances the owner had no choice in the matter because either he had accepted a grant for a major repair, and opening to the public was a condition attached to the grant, or he had been forced, on the death of his father, to apply to the Treasury for 'conditional exemption' from death duties, under the terms of which the house, contents and grounds had to be on view so many days a year to the general public.

Owners who resigned themselves and opened for these reasons sometimes invested considerable capital sums in trying to make opening into a money-making business – only to find, after a number of years of losing substantial sums of money, they would have been better off if they had coughed up the cash to the Treasury and never gone into the business.

The reasons for the failure of many houses was simple. The cost of setting the whole thing up in the first place was high. The public, it seemed, demanded tarmac roads, 'toilet facilities', restaurants, etc. – all extremely expensive; on top of all this, the staffing and extra running costs where often ruinous and far exceeded the amount coming in. Even worse, unless you could demonstrate to the Inland Revenue that you were actively trying to make a profit (in which case you needed to make a profit at least once every five years) the running costs of the house could not be set off against tax. This is why, gradually, many houses have been slowly restricting opening times, or have shut down to the general public totally and gone into yet another venture – corporate entertaining. This – for some – has proved a good wheeze. The caveat though is that, once again, to make serious money you need to be near large centres of population.

Other businesses tried, with varying degrees of success, have been wildlife parks, children's adventure playgrounds, and so on. Many of these went well at first but recently problems have arisen. The public is becoming increasingly sophisticated and demands better and larger attractions every year. Owners find that in order to continue to attract punters they are having to make major investments on an annual basis in new rides, animals, etc. In other words to keep the business going the profits have to be ploughed back.

But whatever business a house owner decided, or does decide, to go into, the location of the property was, and is, the key to the success or failure of it. If you live in a house forty minutes or so away from London or in the Midlands then opportunities abound but if you live out in the sticks then frankly you might as well forget the whole thing and put the money into the stock market.

It is the case that, over the last fifty years, stately-home owners have invested many millions of pounds in commercialising their properties. At the best about a dozen have made regular taxable profits; most of the remainder would probably, with the benefit of hindsight, have been a lot better off putting all their available spare cash into the stock market. As for those poor saps who actually sold property and land in order to raise the necessary capital to open their houses, all I can say is they made a very bad deal indeed.

Not only has the loss of precious capital caused the sale of the house itself, as happened to Lord Brownlow at Belton, but also the pressures of commercialisation and the need to try and make money have destroyed the very ambience and setting which the owner was trying to save for his family. I often recall the words of an American officer in Vietnam who, when asked by a reporter, during the Tet offensive of 1968, why he had just blasted some village off the face of the earth, replied: 'We had to destroy the village in order to save it.' An unfortunate remark, which got relayed round the world rapidly and did the American military PR machine no good at all. Yet many country-house owners seem to follow his advice. They open their house to the public, have various events in their park on a regular basis, hold great corporate functions in their state rooms and end up by moving out and living in the stables or a nearby farmhouse. All this is done in the name of 'saving' the house, but in fact all they have achieved is to turn what was a home into a cross between a sterile museum and an up-market Trusthouse Forte Hotel. The words of the American officer are just as apt, far from the battlefields of Vietnam.

Frankly I am of the unenterprising school of country-house owner. I am aware of the ironical joke that, as we have seen, in spite of all this enterprise many of these operations don't make much money and some actually lose it. In fact, it is doubtful whether even those who do claim to make a substantial trading profit would do so if they put in a charge for the cost of the capital invested in upgrading kitchens, roads, loos and the like to cater for the needs of the public. The most horrifying test would be to see what that capital would have done if invested in the stock market, as opposed to what has been achieved through all this supposed 'enterprise' and effort.

In short, there is much to be said for doing nothing. Those who have practised the 'do nothing' school of country-house and estate management have been among the most successful owners since the war. Sitting on their estates and shivering in front of log fires, they have seen their assets steadily increase in value, their income rise, and now, for the first time for perhaps a century, they can look at their future with a degree of equanimity and, just occasionally, give themselves a treat and turn on the central heating.

In recent years two other instruments have been created by the government in an effort to enable owners to fund their houses – Charitable Trusts and Maintenance Funds. At present there are around twenty large houses owned and supported by Charitable Trusts which have been endowed by the owners. The big advantage is that as charities they are exempt from direct taxation. Some of the largest houses in the land are now owned by such trusts, including Chatsworth, Arundel Castle and Burghley House. Charitable Trusts though are not a panacea for all owners of such properties. For a start the donor loses control, as the majority of the trustees must be independent. Secondly, the family must have sufficient assets to endow the charity at the outset. Thirdly, the remaining assets must be large enough to provide for the family's normal economic needs.

As we shall see when we look at the National Trust it is likely that 'chunky money' would be required for an endowment for even a medium-sized country house and, as the main reason why an owner is struggling in the first place is that he does not have 'chunky money', the large sums required have meant that only a small number of owners have felt able, or willing, to take this route.

I suspect that one other reason for the lack of enthusiasm on the part of many owners for the Charitable Trust route is a feeling that it is some sort of surrender, that they are giving up their freedom to manage their patrimony, if you like, for a mess of pottage.

An alternative solution is the setting up of a Maintenance Fund. In this case the assets vested in the fund are free of the dreaded Inheritance Tax (IHT), but the income is taxed. The income from the fund can only be used for the maintenance of the house and the fund dissolves on the death of the settlor. When this happens his heir can either opt to set it up again – in which case he will avoid IHT on the assets – or wind it up when he would pay IHT. However the attractions of the Maintenance Fund would seem not to be powerful enough to encourage a large number of owners to opt for it and only around sixty have so far been set up.

Needless to say, to opt either to be a Charitable Trust or to set up a Maintenance Fund would involve large professional fee bills. To me it seems the height of injustice that owners, in order to safeguard something which the government insists is part of the National Heritage, are forced to go through a series of convoluted hoops which benefit no one except the lawyers or life insurance companies.

The lack of take-up by most owners of these options speaks for itself. Perhaps like me they dislike intensely the surrender of independence attendant upon these schemes and prefer to gamble on getting their tax planning 'right on the night' – and, if they fail, and the contents of their house are sold and end up overseas, the house broken up into flats, the park turned into a golf course, the farmhouses sold to weekenders, and the nation laments at yet another 'heritage disaster story', then so be it. After all, if 'the nation' really wanted to help, all it has to do is abolish IHT, and anyway what *has* 'the nation' ever done for owners of the so-called National Heritage? Nothing – unless you consider various vague efforts to staunch the flow of blood caused in the first place by 'the nation's' own taxation policies!

CHAPTER 3

The Big House – the Public Sector

The National Trust (NT) was founded in 1894 as a reaction to the danger presented by the growing urban sprawl of late Victorian England; its aim was to secure beauty spots and other areas of the countryside to act – as one of the founders put it – as 'open-air sitting-rooms for the poor'. A hundred and four years on, it is now the UK's largest private landowner and has a membership of over two million.

Although it accepted its first house, Barrington Court in Somerset, in 1907, and took over Montacute in 1931, it was Lord Lothian's address in 1934 which started the ball rolling. By the end of World War II the National Trust had accumulated twenty-three houses and by 1950 this had risen to forty-two; it now has some two hundred and seven houses of various shapes, sizes and description, which are open to the public. These are not all by any manner of means great houses or even country houses, but just over a hundred of them would probably fit the general criteria of a 'country house'.

The increase in National Trust ownership owed much to legislation passed by the post-war Labour government in response to the Gower Report, which finally allowed owners to do what Lord Lothian had urged in 1934 – pass their houses and contents over to the Treasury in lieu of tax; the Treasury then made the property over to the National Trust. Initially this 'relief' was restricted to buildings and land but in 1953 the Conservative government extended it to cover contents.

Over the years many owners considered that the National Trust was the only option available to secure the survival of their property and its continuation as a residence for the family, albeit as tenants rather than owners.

To the casual observer the main difference between a big

house still in private hands and one managed and owned by the National Trust or English Heritage may be that, superficially, the publicly owned properties look in rather more immaculate nick than the majority of those still owned privately. This is true. Both the National Trust and English Heritage have very high standards but then they also have very deep pockets and do not suffer from the trauma of having large slices of their income and capital removed by the taxman at regular intervals.

It is often the case that the richer you are the more lavish and uncontrolled your expenditure and it has to be said that the National Trust is no stranger to this phenomenon. This may indeed be the right place to insert what the National Trust considers a reasonable annual budget for repairs to one of its houses. Admittedly the table on the facing page was drawn up in 1990. I expect the figures have been subject to 'uplift' since then.

Oh, the delights of wallowing in money! The table, it must be remembered, does not refer to a true mega-house of Blenheim Palace, Burghley or Chatsworth proportions but to an average-sized country house. It also, of course, just refers to capital expenditure, not the day-to-day running costs of staff wages, heating, electricity and minor maintenance.

I doubt if very many of the private owners of such properties spend a tithe of that amount per annum on their houses. Hardly surprising when, if you think about it, the National Trust is budgeting to spend, in 1990 pounds, £12.7 million on this property over a hundred-year period; makes you think, doesn't it! It certainly makes my proposal in the preceding chapter that the government should grant owners of listed properties a de-preciation allowance of £100 per square foot, to be amortised over a hundred-year period, a pretty modest request. Incidentally, I wouldn't mind the job of caretaker, with my flat being redone every fifteen years at a cost of £60,000! This is considerably more than my family have spent on redecorating our house over the last hundred years.

But you take my point, I trust, so next time you make an unfavourable comparison between a National Trust property and a private house just bear the above figures in mind.

CAPITAL REPAIRS – AVERAGE ANNUAL COST
(Long-term estimate, allowing for cyclical items)

Major works	Annual cost	Frequency (years)	Annual average
Structural repairs	£100,000	10	£10,000
Reroofing	£750,000	70	£10,700
Repointing	£700,000	25	£28,000
Joinery repairs (external)	£60,000	30	£2,000
Redecoration (external)	£25,000	5	£5,000
Rewiring (system)	£150,000	25	£6,000
Electrical mains	£30,000	40	£750
Renewal of boilers	£50,000	20	£2,500
Renewal of heating system	£30,000	30	£1,000
Plumbing services	£20,000	40	£500
Fire-detection systems	£10,000	15	£700
Security systems	£10,000	15	£700
Redecoration (internal)	£50,000	10	£5,000
Water mains	£75,000	40	£1,900
Drainage	£100,000	40	£2,500
Lightning conductor	£25,000	20	£1,250
Repairs to garden wall	£20,000	10	£2,000
Conservatory floor	£30,000	20	£1,500
Flat renovation	£60,000	15	£4,000
Restaurant/kitchen	£25,000	10	£2,500
Shop	£5,000	5	£1,000
Drives, paths, car parks	£75,000	10	£7,500
Renovation of cottage	£40,000	30	£1,300
Visitors facilities	£20,000	10	£2,000
TOTAL			£100,300
Add average annual minor works			£15,000
SUBTOTAL			£115,300
Add contingency @ 10%			£11,700
GRAND TOTAL			£127,000

This typical budget was drawn up by the National Trust to construct something called the Chorley Formula. The purpose of the formula was to give the National Trust a means of calculating the size of the endowment needed before it took on any new houses. The National Trust had become increasingly concerned that in the past it had often accepted houses with an inadequate endowment and had 'lost' money as a result. It is perhaps not generally realised that the National Trust only takes on a house if it comes with a large enough chunk of land and money to cover upkeep costs.

The formula used by the National Trust to work out how much money it needs is extremely complicated, as you would expect, and is no doubt based on the old premiss that 'bullshit baffles brains'. I set it out below in all its glory.

Annual property expenditure		X
+ 20% (contingencies 12.5%, improvements 7.5%)		X
+ 20% management fee		X
TOTAL		X
Deduct annual property income:		
Rents (less one third)	X	
Other income	X	X
Annual deficit		X
+ 50% uplift		X
Uplifted deficit		Y
Capitalisation rate		Z%
ENDOWMENT REQUIRED		$\dfrac{£Y \times 100}{Z}$

Most of the headings are self-explanatory. The capitalisation rate is taken after assessing the yield on dividend income on investments, so today it would probably be fair to put that in at 4%. Anyway, I thought the inclusion of the formula would amuse those readers, with houses big or small, who, on a wet after-noon, wished to while away the time working out how big an endowment the National Trust would require to take over their property.

For the National Trust, the endowment required is likely to be so large that it is going to be seriously deterred from taking on any new properties – so, in effect the entire exercise has been a waste of time.

This state of affairs was amply illustrated in 1992 when a black-and-white Tudor timber-framed house called Pitchford Hall came on the market. The National Trust offered to take over the house – but at a price – it wanted eleven million pounds! Of this sum it generously proposed that one million pounds should come from its own resources and the balance from the poor benighted tax-payer. In fairness, two million pounds was going to be used to buy the house and contents from the owners, who had been hard hit by Lloyd's underwriting losses, but that still left a requirement of nine million pounds. So how did the National Trust justify its demands for such a large sum? Well, two and a half million pounds was going to be spent putting the house to rights *à la* National Trust and a further half-million pounds on building visitor facilities, leaving a balance of six million pounds to provide the inevitable endowment fund.

Not surprisingly the taxpayer balked at this generous offer and the house and contents were sold privately – and, I suspect, are now being very well cared for at no public expense.

By now I think you see why it is highly unlikely that the National Trust will ever add to its current portfolio of historic country houses. No private owner is likely to be able to endow their property with sufficient capital assets to tempt the National Trust to take over their property – not unless they either (a) hate their prospective heirs or (b) are extremely rich. Gone are the days when impoverished aristocrats could turn to the National Trust *in extremis* and make over the house and park and a thousand acres or so of farmland in order to ensure the survival of their property. For today if you have sufficient funds to endow your house you are – by definition – rich enough to afford to run it in complete luxury for you own selfish enjoyment.

It is perhaps fortunate that in the last few years rich men have recovered their appetite for such properties; very few large country houses nowadays could be considered in danger of dereliction and eventual demolition. That this was not the case back in the glory days of the National Trust, just after the last war, goes without saying, and without doubt the job it did then was superb. But in those far off days the National Trust was run by gentlemen amateurs; now we are subject to the formulas of the bullshit-baffles-brains variety and the grip of the professional manager has extended even to such a quintessential English institution as the National Trust.

In those halycon days, of course, owners who gifted their house to the National Trust often got very good deals indeed. The concept was simple. The nation preserved an historically important house and – usually – the contents, which it acquired for nothing. In return the owner and his family continued to live in the home of their ancestors. Some ignorant commentators now criticise these deals as being too 'generous to the owners'. But such criticism is misplaced for several reasons. First, like all criticisms of past deals, it is made with the benefit of hindsight, and the critic forgets that if the National Trust made a bad deal then it is probably equally true that the heirs of the donor consider their ancestor made a bad deal as well! What's sauce for the goose is sauce for the gander. Secondly, if the families of the old owners had not continued to reside in the houses then the National Trust would have had the expense of finding full-time caretakers. Last but by no means least, if you compute the capital value of the properties and works of art which the National Trust received free of charge, the continued presence of the family seems a small price to have paid.

Inevitably, not all such arrangements have remained happy. Those owners who gave their houses to the National Trust under the impression that they were dealing with gentlemen have now found, to their horror, that that is no longer the case. The result has been a certain amount of friction between donor families and the National Trust, which sometimes spills into the press and affords everyone a certain amount of amusement.

The most common cause of clashes seems to be on the subject of taste. Taste is something most gentlemen feel they have in abundance and are amazed when the National Trust spends a small fortune on getting some poofy interior-design consultant down from London to advise on the colour of the paintwork – they are even more amazed when they see the result, and sometimes burst into print in a fury.

Friction is also caused by the differing views on what a house is. An owner has no difficulty with a house being a place to live in, but the National Trust sometimes views houses as 'time capsules' or, alternatively, as a place in which to recreate the style of living contemporary with the period of the building. This, as often as not, leads to the banishment of any anachronistic object. The consequence is that all too often an air of sterility hangs over these houses. The architect William Clough-Ellis summed up the National Trust's notion of an historic house as: 'a museum in which are preserved, here and there, carefully selected and ticketed items of what England was'.

A classic instance, recorded by David Littlejohn in *The Fate of the English Country House,* is the experience of Lord Scarsdale at Kedleston. In 1987, he wrote to David Littlejohn:

> All I can say is that everything you have heard about their [the National Trust's] amateurishness, waste of money, lack of supervision of staff and contractors, purism, museumisation of the house, coupled with arrogance and lack of courtesy towards the 'donor family' (as they call us), has been repeated and suffered by us here! The National Trust makes it clear they regard us as some sort of thorn in their flesh which they propose rudely to ignore.

Later, in conversation with David Littlejohn, he outlined a veritable catalogue of complaints against the Trust, casting doubts on their choice of colour schemes, deploring their removal of pictures and furniture from public rooms which they considered to be 'out of keeping' with the house, and so on. A typical example given by Lord Scarsdale, and recorded by David Littlejohn, concerned a stand of Wellingtonia redwoods, planted in 1852 to commemorate the death of the great duke. The National Trust wanted to cut them down – 'because they weren't here in 1760!'

Such criticisms are not the sole preserve of Lord Scarsdale but are echoed by many other 'donor families' – so what's gone wrong with the National Trust?

Undoubtedly one of its problems is its success. Its sheer size has caused it to resemble some large corporation with a headquarters which is no longer able to control the operations in the field. Rather like a dinosaur, its body has outgrown its brain. Also like many other flourishing organisations it has forgotten what made it successful in the first place. I have noticed how companies which grow from nothing to become large and successful often owe their success to brilliant quirky individuals who, without any educational or professional qualifications, create highly prosperous businesses. What happens next? Why they announce that in future they will only employ graduates or MBAs, forgetting completely that the company reached its present level precisely because it didn't employ such people!

As with large companies, so with the National Trust. The days of gentleman amateurs, like James Lees-Milne, are over and the organisation is stuffed with so-called experts. Experts are – by definition – arrogant and fanatical about what they see as their field of expertise; they are also – by definition again – surprisingly lacking in that vital component for dealing with people – commonsense.

But the National Trust experts also suffer from the curse of purism that is presently manifesting itself throughout rural Britain. Kedleston is a typical victim of this disease of the experts, in that they want to turn it back into a 'pure' Adam house. To achieve their aim they plan to banish anything which is of a later date and could detract from the 'purity' of the design. This approach is fine for a museum, but country houses are not museums, they are – or, in the case of National Trust-owned properties, were – living breathing developing *homes*. That the development of a country house ceases the day the National Trust takes control is perhaps inevitable, but to try to turn the clock back and remove all traces of the couple of hundred years between a house being built and being given to the National Trust is arrogant and wrong-headed. After all, it is hardly likely that the original builder wanted to freeze, in perpetuity, his design and not allow future generations to improve on it or to hang their own portraits on the walls.

A further mistake of the National Trust is the lengths to which it goes to 'preserve' items which were never intended to be 'preserved'. Threadbare curtains are conserved at great cost, without thought being given to whether (a) the original purchaser might – quite possibly – have made a gross mistake in the first place, balls-ups in interior decorating surely not being a purely twentieth-century phenomenon, or whether (b) their survival is only due to lack of funds by previous owners to replace them. A classic instance of this was the £160,000 the National Trust spent over eleven years restoring the king's bed at Knole; now if I had been the lucky owner of that particular bed, I would have popped down to the Kings Road to an up-market fabric shop, bought some replacements and put the old hangings on the bonfire. Perhaps the most ludicrous example of this approach by National Trust has been the meticulous restoration of Uppark, which was destroyed by fire. New wallpapers were meticulously aged to replicate the ones they were replacing.

However, first prize for total stupidity in the restoration business must go to English Heritage, which is planning to spend a million pounds on 'restoring' the ruin of Wigmore Castle on the Welsh Borders. It was once the home of the mighty Mortimers, the most famous of whom was lover to Edward II's wife and ended up being executed in a particularly revolting fashion – which was fair enough in a way as he had had Edward II killed by shoving a red-hot poker up his bottom. But I digress. English Heritage proposes carefully to remove vegetation, such as ivy, from the walls – make them good – and then let the ivy grow back! Keen 'conservationists' will be even more impressed to hear that when English Heritage remove grass and moss, etc. from the ramparts and the tops of the walls to make essential repairs, every effort will be made to 'save' the same vegetation and to encourage it to grow back on the repaired part of the wall!

Needless to say, the cost of adopting such a 'purist' approach to the interiors of many houses, or, as in the case of Wigmore, the exteriors, has meant that the cost of managing them has got out of control and has contributed to the advent of the Chorley Formula, which – as we have seen – effectively means that the National Trust are unlikely to take over any other large houses in the future.

One has to conclude by saying that the National Trust today seems to have become a rather aimless organisation in comparison with what it was forty years ago. Its very success has caused this. In the old days, with travel difficult and only a small and knowledgeable membership, it could afford to work for the preservation of buildings and landscapes; now, with its membership over two million, it has a problem balancing the often conflicting aims of conservation and public access.

The furore over Avebury is a case in point. The Trust acquired Avebury Manor and the surrounding land after a protracted campaign by the local people, who were frightened that some unscrupulous developer would purchase the estate and try to commercialise the village and the prehistoric stone circle. What has been the result? Why the saviours are now the villains. The National Trust want to build a 'visitors' centre' with 'an interpretation room'. In other words they want to encourage more people to come to Avebury – the very thing the locals did not want to happen! And the organisation they put their trust in has effectively kicked them in the balls.

So what is the solution? Perhaps the National Trust should consider following the example of many large companies, who have found themselves in a similar situation, and devolve power and responsibilities down to subsidiaries, or in their case to the regions. Undoubtedly the main cause of its current problems is its sheer monolithic size, and among the *cognoscenti* its performance is unfavourably contrasted with its sister, but independent, organisation, the National Trust for Scotland.

In any case, perhaps the National Trust should change its name, for, although it is many things, one thing it is not is trustworthy. This unpalatable fact was recently apparent when the National Trust banned stag-hunting on its land on Exmoor, even though the donor of most of its acreage there had specifically expressed the wish that stag-hunting should be allowed to continue on the land. By banning hunting the National Trust demonstrated to all countrymen that it is not an organisation that can any longer be trusted and has thrown in its lot with all those other bodies whose sole aim seems to be the sterilisation and 'Disneyfication' of the countryside. Many people expressed surprise at the National Trust's action, but if they had talked to the many poor sods who still live in houses which their fathers trustingly gave away to the National Trust they would have realised that the National Trust is a very different body today from what it was in the 1950s and 1960s.

The conflict between preservation and public access is not going to go away and we will come back to it later. Indeed, the two aims are too often incompatible and one day the issue will need to be addressed not just by the National Trust but also by the National Parks and English Heritage.

CHAPTER 4

The Contents

If people only knew as much about painting
as I do they would never buy my pictures.

SIR EDWIN LANDSEER (1802–73)

Big houses have contents. This fairly basic fact is, strangely, frequently forgotten by people when they are buying a large house – let alone a stately home. There is nothing more pitiful than wandering around one with a new owner and seeing it virtually naked, stripped not only of the good furniture, pictures and books but also of the clutter which gradually accumulates over a few hundred years. Furnishing a big house from scratch is an expensive business and the wise buyer should, mentally, add at least a million pounds on to the asking price to allow for it before buying one.

The contents of big houses, as it happens, have played a very large part in ensuring the survival of many estates. Pictures and furniture acquired casually over the centuries with no particular aim in mind except to furnish the house, have, to the delight of many owners, become objects of enormous value, eagerly sought after by the new rich.

It would be fair to say that, without the acquisitive streak which, luckily, the eighteenth-century ancestors of most families appear to have possessed, the number of estates and large houses still in private hands would be far fewer today. It was also fortunate that this craze to collect and beautify their houses was mainly an eighteenth-century phenomenon, for that was a century when not only were art and good taste at their peak (it is hard to think of a single thing produced in the eighteenth century which is not beautiful) but also a time when the fortunes of Britain's landed families were at their zenith.

Indeed the British golden guinea was so valuable abroad that those who had foolishly overspent their income in the UK repaired to the continent to live cheaply in luxury while allowing the rents at home to accumulate and pay off their debts. At the same time it was – conveniently – a period when the fortunes of Italian aristocrats were at an all-time low.

One other factor must be added – Latin. The study of classics – Latin and Greek – was *de rigeur* for anyone who had aspirations to being thought educated in the eighteenth century. (Not only then, of course; the author spent many useless and boring hours trying to master the language at school, with a total lack of success, back in the 1960s.) The veneration accorded to Latin and all things classical led naturally to sending your boy on the Grand Tour to complete his education. And when in Rome, Florence or Venice the opportunity to buy art was an ever-present temptation. So perhaps Latin was not such a useless language to learn after all, as its popularity as a means of disciplining the minds of the young in the eighteenth century led, indirectly, to the accumulation of quantities of old master paintings in Britain's country houses which many owners have been happily living off for the last seventy-odd years.

It is a myth that prices of fine art rise ineluctably; the reality is rather different. Art is a creature of fashion. At various times the *objets d'art* of certain periods and styles are in vogue and their prices rise to stratospheric levels, while, conversely, unfashionable forms of art are considerably undervalued. The valuation of art depends little on its quality but much on whether it is *à la mode* among those who have both the money and the desire to build up collections.

Examples of this abound. In the late nineteenth century, early English oak furniture was top of the pops and, a little later, the price paid for eighteenth-century mezzotints and engravings of English portraits reached unprecedented levels – superb examples routinely selling, in the early twentieth century, for figures of around a thousand pounds or, in modern money, sixty thousand plus. Today you could probably pick up similar-quality prints for roughly the same sum in nominal terms.

When Britain's aristocrats found themselves on their uppers

after the First World War, what was then the fashionable thing to buy were the very things they had most of – English eighteenth-century portraits and Italian old masters. As far as the buyers were concerned – rich Americans – these were the greatest examples of the art of painting in the world and thus fetched staggering prices. Dealers like the notorious Duveen made a fortune introducing rich Americans to impoverished – and sometimes not so impoverished – British aristocrats who were only too willing to part with family portraits for what, at the time, seemed astronomical sums. It was a shrewd move on their part for, except in rare circumstances, eighteenth-century British portraits have fallen dramatically in value in real terms over the last sixty-odd years as the tastes of the mega-rich have turned to French Impressionists and Post Impressionists.

In fact, the last sixty-odd years have seen an 'action replay' of the eighteenth century. Then it was the English 'milord' whose wealth staggered the continentals and it was the Italian aristocrats who were poor and eager to sell. Since the 1930s it has been rich Americans who have been able to buy from the impoverished descendants of these English and Scottish gentlemen.

The excitement caused among British owners by the arrival of the 'wall of money' from America dedicated to buying art in the early twentieth century is hard to exaggerate. This quote from a letter from my father, then a young officer in the army, to his mother in 1933 gives a flavour:

> I saw Symonds who asked if I had a Jourdains picture – I said I thought so but was not certain. He has got a rich Yank, Howard I. Young, who buys pictures for large sums, ten thousand pounds, etc. He said he wanted a Jourdains . . . He would like to bring H. I. Young over and show it to him . . .

The readiness of the British to sell art was boosted by the fact that many of them had a large surplus of the stuff. As part of the aristocratic retrenchment caused by confiscatory taxation and depressed rental income, large town houses in London were being sold and demolished and replaced by office blocks and subsidiary country houses were being closed down and leased to institutions or demolished. The result was that owners could sell off their 'surplus art' without actually denuding their principal residence.

Not that the sale of art from country houses was a new phenomenon. In previous centuries suddenly impoverished aristocrats had often sold off pictures and libraries. What was new was that now virtually every landowner felt he was poor and needed cash, so that every picture in the country was effectively for sale at the right price. Even the Duke of Westminster was persuaded to part with Gainsborough's *Blue Boy* when offered £150,000 for it by Henry Huntington.

There are few owners who have not, over the last sixty or so years, yielded to the temptation to solve their financial problems by flogging the odd picture, piece of furniture or item of jewellery. Actually, ironically, it does not always solve them. There is something about an overdraft which makes it very difficult to get rid of. I remember once when I was having lunch at my club someone sat down and announced to all and sundry that he had finally persuaded his wife to part with the tiara and he had popped it at Christies for a large sum, thus paying off the overdraft. We all congratulated him till a wise old bird at the end of the table said: 'I bet you've got the overdraft back now!' There was a moment's silence; then it was admitted that the overdraft had indeed mysteriously returned. Flush with riches they had had an expensive holiday, he had bought a new car and a new suit, they had a done up a couple of rooms, made over some money to some undeserving daughter and – hey presto – they were back to square one – but now they had no tiara left to sell.

That is the trouble with having 'windfall money' in the bank. Few landowners have ever, in their entire lives, had the luxury of a bulging bank account, so when it does finally bulge the temptation to go on a bit of a spending binge is hard to resist – as incidentally are the demands from your family to help them out now you have finally sold the picture, tiara or whatever.

As time went by, the export of art from the UK across the Atlantic was partially stemmed by a mixture of measures. First, in 1952 the government introduced what is known as the Waverley Formula. When applied, this means that if a work of art is considered of 'national importance' an export licence can be denied for a 'reasonable time' to allow a British museum or art gallery time to collect sufficient money to match the price offered and thus 'save' the picture for the nation.

Another device employed is 'Conditional Exemption'. This may be invoked at the owner's death and means that the Treasury agrees not to charge death duties or, as it is known as today, Inheritance Tax, on a work of art which is considered to be of 'museum quality' or to be an 'historically associated object'. The item then normally remains *in situ* on condition that it is available, at the very least, for public viewing on request.

A great number of families have made use of this exemption over the years and the *Register of Conditionally Exempt Works of Art* now consists of over sixteen thousand items. This vast amount of art must be worth at least an average of fifty thousand pounds per item, giving an overall value to the registered works of well over a billion pounds. Back in the early 1990s there was a bit of a row in Parliament about the fact that many of these 'exempt' works were tucked away in private houses not open to the public, and that few people knew about them, let alone how to gain access to them. Actually the critics were wrong as the *Register* is freely available on request from the various museums and galleries which keep a copy. And the critics also conveniently ignored the fact that only a fraction of the art owned by 'the nation' is on show at any one time. The basements of the National Gallery and the Tate, for instance, are simply stuffed with pictures for which there is no hanging space available, and the government's own 'private' art collection which is used to decorate the offices and residences of ministers of the crown, embassies, etc. accounts for another sizeable chunk.

Apart from public access, the main catch to Conditional Exemption comes if you ever sell the picture. First, you have to pay Capital Gains Tax (CGT) on it (as you do with any high-value object you sell) but, in addition, you will be liable to pay death duties on what remains after CGT, at the rate prevailing when the object was exempted. For those poor sods whose father died at the wrong time, when death duties touched eighty per cent for estates over a million pounds in value, this effectively means they cannot ever sell them, as the 'dividend' would be pathetically small.

To give a rough example. Say your father died in 1953, when rates were at their height and left an estate of well over a million pounds. In order to reduce the tax bill a picture worth £25,000 was accepted by the Treasury as conditionally exempt; now, forty-four years later, you realise its value is a million pounds and you examine whether it is worth selling. First you will pay CGT on the net figure so your calculation will look something like this:

Hammer price	£1,000,000
Less cost of sale	– £100,000
Less market value on 31/3/82	– £200,000
So chargeable gain since 1982	£700,000
Less indexation allowance, say (*the value, for CGT is indexed to allow for inflation*)	– £150,000
Leaving a gain for CGT of	£550,000
Less CGT payable @ 40%	– £220,000
Leaving a figure of	£330,000
Now pay death duties @ 80% on what's left	– £264,000
Residue left to spend – the princely sum of	£66,000

Actually you would be extremely stupid to sell under the above circumstances. 'Conditional Exemption' only lasts for your lifetime; on your death, your heir has to reapply. If it is then granted again, the exemption will be at the then current rate of IHT (at present forty per cent).

Gallingly, the responsibility for insuring and maintaining these objects, although, as the above calculation shows, they are effectively ninety-two-per-cent 'owned' by the Treasury, remains one hundred per cent the responsibility of their nominal 'owner'! This raises, for me, an interesting question. Suppose the object is stolen or destroyed in a fire; as you have been paying the premiums you pick up the sum insured, and as the object has been destroyed and not sold the state cannot claim its share. Of course, you would be subject to tax on the insurance payout – unless that is you bought something with the money to replace the object, which would then be yours totally if you ever had to sell it.

It is surely an anomaly that owners insure their works of art, and pay hefty premiums on them for their 'replacement value'; when so much of the market value, in the event of sale, is going to be taken by the government in the form of Capital Gains Tax, why, I wonder, should owners effectively insure the Treasury's interest in their works of art? After all, you may have a Van Dyck portrait of an ancestor valued at a million pounds; it is irreplaceable so in the event of its being stolen or burnt you cannot 'replace' it. Surely you should only be expected to insure your interest in the picture and, in the event of disaster, you should not be taxed on the insurance money, even if you decide to pocket the cash and not roll it over into a new work of art?

Another device often made use of by owners is 'Heritage Sales'. This is either the sale of an object to an 'approved body', like the National Trust or a museum, or to the Treasury in return for tax concessions.

Such sales are conducted by private treaty. The advantages for an owner of such a transaction is that it is totally exempt from all capital taxes. As a result, though the 'the approved bodies' take this into account when offering to buy, and thus the owner receives a significantly lower gross sum for his work of art, he may end up with a higher net figure than if he had sold through the auction houses and had to pay CGT and perhaps IHT on the deal.

The first step in negotiating a private-treaty sale is that the seller and the 'approved body' have to come to an agreement on what the 'open market' price of the object would be. The next step is to calculate what the seller's tax liability would be if he sold on the open market at that price.

The following example from Sotheby's *Management of Works of Art* will make the advantages clear.

Value of work of art	£100,000
Less CGT @ 40% of say £20,000	– £8,000
Leaving	£92,000
Less IHT @ 40%	– £36,800
Leaving	£55,200

So if the owner sold on the open market he would be left, after all capital taxation, with £55,200. If, on the other hand, he did a private-treaty sale he would be credited with a *douceur* worth 25% of the CGT bill and 25% of IHT bill; in other words, his tax bill would be significantly reduced and, in the example above, he would receive an extra £11,200.

There is one further advantage of the system which makes it particularly attractive to owners – the purchasing body may well decide to let the object remain *in situ,* if the house is open to the public and it is considered to have important historical connections with the building. In other words, not only does the owner pocket more cash but he also gets – more often than not – continued possession of the work of art.

Such then is the theory. The problem comes with agreeing the initial 'open market' valuation. The tax advantages on offer are only of use if the valuation is at the right price. If the two parties cannot agree to it then an owner may still be substantially better off selling through an auction house and gambling that his advisers have got it right and that the price obtained is going to be vastly higher than what the museums were prepared to agree on. This, it must said, has often been the case. The most spectacular example was the sale by the Duke of Devonshire of old-master drawings which ended up fetching at auction several times the British Museum's estimate of what their 'market value' was.

The calculation for selling an object in lieu of tax are exactly the same as for a Heritage Sale.

The end result of all these measures is that the flood tide of sales has been stemmed somewhat.

Of course, the key to the valuation – in the case of a painting –

is the identity of the painter. This is an obvious but often disregarded point. As an example of the importance of getting this right take the case of the Duke of Devonshire who settled part of his immense death-duty bill by giving a Rembrandt to the National Gallery – the joke was that some years later the experts decided it wasn't a Rembrandt after all, but by then the deal had been done.

Owners would do well to remember this as a cautionary tale. If you are thinking of selling something, it is as well to tout it round as many experts as possible in the search for the one who will give it the best attribution. Experts in art being no different from those in any other field, as often as not they will be in total disagreement. On the other hand, when valuing for probate, the last thing you want is your things to be 'overvalued' because of optimistic attributions – unless, that is, you are planning to use the valuation as a base figure when asking the Treasury to accept the painting in lieu of taxes.

Country-house owners have been both the beneficiaries and the victims of the surge in art prices. It is true they can raise large sums of money by selling works of art but, at the same time, they are heavily taxed on inflated values if their father dies in possession of them.

In fact, it is a moot point whether an owner should be pleased or saddened at being informed that a picture that for years has been a source of enjoyment to him is now considered to be by, say, Van Dyck, and thus worth a million pounds – rather than being, as had previously been thought, just 'School of Van Dyck', and thus worth only ten thousand pounds. It is the same picture, it is just that an 'expert' has now changed the attribution and with it the value. Now the poor owner has to consider the insurance and the security of it and whether he can justify having a million pounds tied up in a canvas hanging on the wall. The answer, probably, is no, so up it goes to London for sale.

The real problem with works of art from an owner's viewpoint is that they are virtually valueless as a means of producing income. So any sensible owner will always sell a picture rather than a farm. After all, if you sell a picture for enough money you can probably pay the debts off and have enough change left over to buy a replacement to hang in the empty space and, who knows, in fifty years' time that replacement picture may well be worth more than what was sold off the wall in the first place as the school of art it came from suddenly becomes flavour of the year in the art market.

The dribble of works of art from country houses will continue as long as Inheritance Tax is charged on them. The burden of IHT will increase as works of art - on the whole - increase in value due to scarcity. In short, a vicious circle is created with only one way of breaking it - the abolition of capital taxation on death.

CHAPTER 5

The Park and Gardens

Our England is a garden that is full of stately views,
Of borders, beds and shrubberies and lawns and avenues,
With statues on the terraces and peacocks strutting by;
But the Glory of the Garden lies in more than meets the eye.

RUDYARD KIPLING (1865-1936)

The central and most visible sign of an estate may be the big house, but the first indication we have that we are in the vicinity of one is a striking change in the character of the landscape. Rolling fields are replaced by what look like the remains of some great forest, with ancient trees dotted over an expanse of verdant grassland. You know at once that you are passing by the park of some great house, and eagerly peer through the trees to try and catch a glimpse of the mansion itself.

I have two heroes as far as park and gardens are concerned – Capability Brown and the anonymous character who invented the weedkiller Round Up; let me explain.

Before Capability Brown arrived on the scene most houses boasted elaborate gardens replicating, with their complicated parterres and formal, architect-designed layouts, the type perfected by Louis XIV's gardener, Le Notre. Everyone will be familiar with gardens of this sort; they are frequently depicted in the kind of seventeenth-century pictures of houses known as 'bird's eye views', and very attractive they must have been, too – providing, of course, you were a bird. Because it is a peculiarity of these grandiose designs that they can really only be appreciated by someone flying over them. From ground level they are just so many miles of gravel paths and clipped hedges. One is forced to the conclusion that garden-design experts in the seventeenth century were extremely clever salesmen; the plans of the garden they proposed – no doubt complete with the proverbial 'bird's eye view' – would have looked very impressive on paper and the poor sucker of a client would have forgotten, in his enthusiasm, that he was not a bird. By the time he realised his mistake it would be to late, the garden would have been planted and the bills paid. Then his only option would have been to pretend he was a satisfied customer and to boast to his friends about his great gardens.

Capability Brown's novel concept was to realise his clients couldn't fly and to plan his gardens to look brilliant from eye level. But his true genius, as far as we, the inheritors of his work, are concerned, was to abolish formal gardens. Instead, he replaced them with parks. Parks, moreover, which swept right up to the front of the house. The reason of course why we bless his name so feelingly is that parks require little maintenance – the odd tree needs replacing, it is true, but on the whole animals mow the grass for nothing, so the park achieves the twin aims of making a house look grand while at the same time costing only a minimal amount to keep up.

I often wonder, when I sweep down a drive through rolling parkland, what Capability Brown would have created if he had had at his disposal the full range of modern earth-moving equipment? Would he still have restricted himself to working within the natural contours of the countryside, or would he have brought up rank upon rank of bright yellow monster machines and created great valleys and hills in the flat landscapes of much of England?

Of course, many parks are but a shadow of their former great selves. Our Edwardian and Victorian ancestors enjoyed them when they were at their peak, but considering perhaps, rather in the manner of today's ignorant environmentalists, that trees live forever, they neglected to plant replacements. The result of their neglect, married with the ploughing up of parkland in the First and Second World Wars, was the virtual disintegration of many fine landscapes. It is only in the last thirty-odd years that owners have begun to repair the damage, and it will, as ever with trees, be our grandsons who reap the benefit.

The need of estate owners to 'maximise income' has also led to parks becoming much smaller. As the home farm grew, covetous eyes were cast over vistas of 'unimproved' grassland, and all too often they were taken in hand to provide yet more arable acres. A cursory visit to many an estate will find the odd remaining grand tree standing forlornly in acres of golden wheat or dank brown plough, a sad reminder of what once was and could be again – if the owner could afford to forgo the income now being derived from what was his park.

Of course the dreaded 'flower garden' has crept back into fashion since the days of Capability Brown and now most big houses will boast one. Personally, I put this down to the increasing influence of the female of the species, who likes colour and nice smells. So some of the park has had to be ploughed up to produce an income which is spent on employing a gardener to look after the flower garden. I would suggest most houses would benefit from abolishing the flower garden and restoring the park; however, few wives would agree to such an obvious course of action, so we are, I am afraid, stuck with flowers.

Which of course is where my second hero, the anonymous inventor of Round Up, comes in. This brilliant product makes gardening a pleasure. All you have to do is put a knapsack-sprayer on your back and wander round your flowerbeds zapping weeds. No more boring hours of hoeing or hand weeding for me. It is true that the occasional plant falls victim to the odd ill-aimed squirt, but that is a small price to pay, although one's wife does not always agree.

Big houses invariably boast the remnants of a vegetable garden. This is usually a walled area of an acre or more. In the days before the advent of the local Tesco and Sainsbury superstore, the 'kitchen garden' provided the household with vegetables and fruit which otherwise were difficult, or impossible, to get hold of. Now, unfortunately, most are grassed over, or perhaps relegated to some humble task like growing Christmas trees. The economics of employing a Mr McGregor to provide home-grown vegetables for the house no longer, alas, make sense. I suppose a modern Mr McGregor would now cost around ten thousand pounds per annum, plus a rent-free cottage, and there is just no way that the average household could possibly eat enough produce to justify, economically, his employment. This is sad as a beautifully maintained walled vegetable garden is as important a part of a country house as old masters, libraries, gleaming silver and rolling open parkland, yet it is an aspect which has been sorely neglected, even by such owners as the National Trust.

There is yet one more kind of garden. The pleasure ground or woodland garden. This is very much the legacy of our Victorian and Edwardian ancestors. Towards the end of the nineteenth century, exotic plants were arriving on our shores, collected by intrepid plant collectors from around the Empire, and many of them were found to flourish in this country, especially on the warm and wet western side. So began an abiding craze for rhododendrons, magnolias, camellias and other exotic shrubs, as well as specimen trees. Such planting and management is normally the preserve of the male of the house and can often be taken to excess.

Many owners forget that the aim of a woodland garden should be to provide a pleasant walk and allow their walks to become the garden equivalent of an art gallery, with specimen after specimen planted in every conceivable piece of open space. In short, they exhibit the classic symptoms of the mad collector. Sadly they can never complete their collection, as plant breeders everywhere are busy developing new types of shrub faster than they can plant them. Walking through such gardens can be a claustrophobic experience, as one is perpetually hemmed in on every side by evergreen plants and never allowed a glimpse of a view. These owners I sometimes feel forget that the primary aim of gardens should be to create something of beauty and interest and that a surfeit of anything is bad for you – even rhododendrons.

Paradoxically, I expect future generations will get a lot of good healthy exercise from cutting down and ripping out shrubs which are now being planted, just as I, today, when I feel in need of exercise, reach for my saw and go and tackle some overgrown laurel or rhododendron. For it has to be said that gardens, both of the flower and woodland variety, serve a valuable purpose. The *nouveaux riches* have their indoor gyms to work off the surplus flab and keep themselves fit, but the gentry have their gardens and shrubberies.

CHAPTER 6

The Land

They love the land because it is their own,
And scorn to give aught other reason why;
Would shake hands with a king upon his throne,
And think it kindness to his majesty.

FITZ-GREENE HALLECK (1790–1867)

If the country house and surrounding park are the heart of an estate then land is surely the blood. Without land a house loses its purpose and becomes just a rich – or perhaps – poor man's – plaything.

Historically one went with the other. When agriculture was booming and rents rising then was the time the landowner could, and more often than not did, indulge his penchant for 'improving' his estates. When the dark shadow of depression and heavy tax burdens fell on the countryside then the squire battened down the hatches and tried, as best he could, to survive. Those that did not, went under.

As we have seen, as early as the fourteenth century an Italian was remarking at the propensity of English merchants to put their ill-gotten gains into land, and the reason was clear. Land not only gave social prestige but it was safe. Having built up a fortune by speculating in the medieval equivalent of financial derivatives, our man wanted to ensure his money was not lost. With few alternative investments available to him, land was the obvious choice. It provided an income while at the same time affording him status. To quote the words which Trollope put into the mouth of Archdeacon Grantley: 'Land gives so much more than rent. It gives one position and influence and political power, to say nothing of game.' It also provided the new owner's sons with an opportunity to matriculate as gentleman and to shake the polluting dust of trade from off their shoes and join the nobility.

The desire to own land was thus, in medieval times, partly driven by economic reasons and partly by the social ambitions of the buyer for his family. Amusingly, exactly the same factors are normally uppermost in the mind of the modern buyer. It seems that as far as land goes nothing ever really changes.

Land remained a good investment right up to the start of the great agricultural depression in 1873, although like all investments it had its ups and downs. By then there were many investment vehicles competing for a rich man's money, vehicles which had multiplied since the advent of government debt in the latter part of the seventeenth century. Kings, of course, had borrowed money from rich subjects before then, but it was hardly a risk-free contract (for the lender, that is) as rulers had an irritating habit of, at the best, reneging on their debts or, at the worst, actually killing the people who had lent them money – as the Order of Templars found out when Pope Clement V abolished them in 1312 and burnt a large number at the stake, or the Jews of England who were summarily expelled from England in 1290 by Edward I.

The financial scandal of the South Sea Bubble in 1720, which burnt a lot of landowners' fingers, convinced them once again that there were only two safe investments – land and government stock. This dictum held good for many years. Land which in 1725 was worth twenty-four years' purchase rose to thirty years' purchase by 1800 and peaked at forty years' purchase in the 1860s. Taking the rent roll and working out the number of years it was going to take, at current rents, to earn back the capital was the accepted method of valuing land back in those days. Doing the same sum today and assuming a rent of £60 per acre we come up with a value, for tenanted land, of £2,400 per acre at forty years' purchase. Land, of course, is no longer a single market but rather a three-tier market. Land with vacant possession is valued more highly, for instance, than land with a pre-1976 tenant (whose heirs have the right of inheritance). Also it must be remembered that back in the eighteenth and nineteenth centuries (and indeed right up to the late 1960s) farmhouses were not greatly valued – it was the land that was important. Now, especially with small farms in scenic landscapes within easy reach of London, it is, more often than not, the house which is sought after and the land is regarded as an incidental amenity rather than an essential income-producing business opportunity. In 1997, farms let on the open market were routinely making over a £100 per acre and, in certain cases, up to £150 an acre, which would give us a price for land, at forty years' purchase, of around £4,000 or £6,000 an acre. Land which attracted such rents, however, was more likely to be fetching £3,500 an acre or, to use the old-fashioned method of valuation, between thirty and thirty-five years' purchase – still some way off its late nineteenth-century peak. In fact, since reliable records began in the late eighteenth century, land has fluctuated between, in modern money terms, £500 and £4,000 an acre. In essence, then, land prices in 1997 were near their peak, and as we contemplate a long tunnel of agricultural recession we can expect them to fall considerably in the short term. However, we must take comfort from the fact that the value of that charming six-bedroom farmhouse will act as a considerable break to a collapse in land prices.

Another factor is that land prices have in the past been inextricably linked to wheat prices and my guess is that the link will continue. For instance, during much of the 1950s right up to the early 1970s land only rose slowly in value to a level of around £500 per acre. Over the same period the price of wheat hovered around £30 per ton. It was not till 1973, when the UK joined the EEC, that the price of wheat – and thus land – began to escalate dramatically. Since then there has been a clear correlation between the price of land and the price of wheat. Of course, in current market conditions (1998), with wheat likely to remain between £70 and £90 a ton for some time, the logical conclusion is that the price of land must fall dramatically from its present height of around £3,000 to £3,500 an acre to around £1,000 to £1,250 an acre. However, this does not take into account Arable Area Aid which is at the moment worth around £90 an acre or between £22 and £30 a ton, depending on the average yield on the land in question. In other words, assuming

Arable Area Aid is likely to continue at its current level, in order to judge what the correct price level of land today should be we have to add around £30 to the price of a ton of wheat and thus arrive at approximately £100 per ton which would indicate that the average price of land should fall to between £1,250 and £1,500 an acre.

But aside from its role as an investment, land has a peculiar characteristic which makes it ideal as a way of storing wealth – it is difficult to sell. Stocks and shares can be flogged by making a simple telephone call but the decision to sell land is just the first step in a long, tortuous – and often painful – process. It also has another major drawback or virtue – it is public. You can gaily flog your entire portfolio of investments and none of your neighbours or friends will be an iota the wiser, but as soon as you put a farm or estate on the market your financial situation becomes public knowledge and a subject of gossip. So land is the last thing anyone likes to sell and many owners cling on to the last in comparative poverty, hoping against hope for some windfall legacy from a distant relation which will save them. Strangely enough it often happens, and the family fortunes are temporarily restored.

Those who doubt this analysis should consider whether there are any descendants of rich merchant families of the fourteenth or fifteenth centuries still surviving on the remnants of what were, then, vast fortunes. The answer is none – unless their ancestor invested in land; there are several hundred landowning families who can trace their current prosperity back to those times and – in some cases – beyond.

The value of land is no different from any other commodity – its price reflects its ability to produce income. For this reason land has always been under threat from government interference. This is nothing new. The provision of food is, after all, essential to our existence. In 1672, and again in 1688, Parliament passed the Corn Bounty Acts, these were designed to discourage imports and boost exports and were measures aimed at stabilising the price of corn at around 48 shillings a quarter or £10.65 a ton! That should make you sit up and think. £10.65 for a ton of wheat in 1688 would be the equivalent of around £1,000 a ton today! A quarter (consisting of eight bushels) was incidentally the normal unit of measure used up till the 1920s for marketing corn. To complicate matters still further, it was a measure of volume rather than of weight; however, approximately four quarters equal one ton.

The price of wheat was to fluctuate wildly as time went by, depending from year to year on whether or not the harvest was good. In the year of Malplaquet (1709) the price reached 75 shillings a quarter, but by 1881, when, we are taught, cheap wheat from America had virtually destroyed English agriculture it was still 48 shilling a quarter – £10.65 a ton – or exactly the same as it had been in 1688! The trouble was, of course, that costs had risen enormously over the previous two hundred years and yields were still pathetically low by modern standards – eighteen hundredweight an acre being the norm against three or four tons today.

The golden period was perhaps 1790 to 1815, when the Napoleonic Wars made imports difficult, and sometimes impossible, at a time when the urban population was expanding rapidly and needed to be fed. Over the twenty-five-year period of the wars, rents increased by between a hundred and two hundred per cent as the price of wheat rocketed; in 1812, it reached 122 shillings a quarter; landowners and farmers invested heavily in new buildings, enclosures and drainage, and much land which had thitherto always been pasture was brought under the plough.

Inevitably the boom ended with the final defeat of Napoleon in 1815. The reason for the slump had little to do – this time – with cheap imports as the Corn Laws, which were passed in 1815, forbade the sale of imported corn on the home market unless the price of wheat exceeded 80 shillings a quarter; this, as a matter of interest, was not to be the case till over a hundred years later in 1920! The fall in prices had more to do with improved arable techniques producing higher yields, the large increase in arable acreage caused by the sky-high prices wheat had reached during the wars and a series of good harvests; all these factors conspired to bring about a crash in prices which the market was not to recover from until around 1837 – a period of recession, oddly, roughly as long as the preceding boom. It is true that the effect was patchy, with many farmers on the light land continuing to make reasonable profits while the marginal arable farms suffered most. Landowners found themselves having to reduce rents in the bad years by between ten and twenty per cent. The net impact on landowners' incomes was relieved by the fact that, with the end of the wars, taxation levels fell and severe deflation set in, reducing wage costs, etc. Those who were worst hit were, as usual, those who had borrowed heavily towards the end of the boom to invest in improvements or in a grandiose new country house.

This propensity farmers and landowners have for over-spending in the good years thus causing the bad years – when they inevitably come – to be far worse than they need be, is repeated so often that one is forced to the conclusion that God, in his infinite wisdom, has programmed man's brain with a self-destruct device to stop individuals from getting too rich. For it is sadly a fact that no one ever learns from history, or from anything else for that matter. The best business advice for land-owners may be found in the Bible, in the Book of Genesis, where Joseph was called to interpret the Pharaoh's dream which the latter described as follows:

> 'And, behold, there came up out of the river seven kine [cattle], fat fleshed and well favoured; and they fed in a meadow.
>
> And, behold, seven other kine came up after them, poor and ill favoured and lean fleshed, such as I never saw in all the land of Egypt for badness.
>
> And the lean and ill-favoured kine did eat up the first seven fat kine.
>
> And when they had eaten them up, it could not be known that they had eaten them; but they were still ill favoured, as at the beginning. So I awoke.'

Joseph interpreted the Pharaoh's dream thus:

> 'The seven good kine are seven years . . . and the seven thin and ill-favoured kine that came up after them are seven years . . .

Behold there come seven years of great plenty throughout all the land of Egypt.

And there shall arise after them seven years of famine; and all the plenty shall be forgotten in the land of Egypt; and famine shall consume the land.'

Pharaoh was so impressed by Joseph's interpretation that he immediately made him the ancient Egyptian equivalent of prime minister and put him charge of arranging storage of one fifth of the harvest during the good years to provide for the lean times ahead.

Time after time we go through agricultural booms and time after time we make the same mistake – spend the money on frivolous things during the good years and have no reserves when the bad years come. Not that landowners are unique in this regard; every business sector acts in the same way.

In any event, come 1835 things began to improve; as an illustration of the roller-coaster nature of the market which then developed, the following figures are for the price of a quarter of wheat in Salisbury market:

November	1835	1836	1837	1838
Price per quarter	36*s*.	60*s*.	58*s*.	72*s*.

It was the dramatic rise in corn prices which caused the pressure from the urban masses for the repeal of the Corn Laws, which eventually happened in 1846. Initially this had little effect on prices, due to a mixture of bad harvests and European revolutions, but in 1850 England was flooded with cheap European grain and the price of wheat dived to 40*s*. a quarter. This was to be a low point; prices gradually recovered and, in fact, over the next thirty years only once touched 40*s*. a quarter again, in 1864. It was not until 1873 that the full horror of falling corn prices was, once more, to hit the landowners.

This was caused by a combination of events and mechanical advances which brought disaster to farmers and landowners. The opening up of the prairies in North America, the expansion of the railway network there, improvements in harvesting technology and faster and bigger ships able to ply the North Atlantic route. All these factors married together led to an avalanche of cheap corn pouring into the UK market and causing enormous distress and economic hardship among farmers.

The following extract from Sir John Fortescue's memoirs *Author and Curator* will give a flavour of the crisis which afflicted agriculture, especially the arable areas, by 1890.

> My father owned in Lincolnshire an estate which had brought him, in good years, a gross income of £7,000 to £8,000 a year. It was all of it reclaimed land, arable; but corn brought no price, the tenants had thrown up their farms, and my father was fain to take them in hand himself. I went through the accounts with him: and we found that instead of a net profit of £4,000 to £5,000 they showed a dead loss of over £2,000. Yet he did not repine. Land once reclaimed – he said – must never be allowed to go back.

In 1894, Oscar Wilde could put these immortal words into the mouth of Lady Bracknell in *The Importance of Being Ernest* and bring the house down: 'What between the duties expected of one in one's lifetime and the duties extracted from one after one's death, land has ceased to be either a profit or a pleasure. It gives one position, and prevents one from keeping it up. That is all that can be said about land.'

By now it was clear that the political map of the United Kingdom had changed and power had switched to the towns. Not even a sympathetic Conservative government could do anything to alleviate the crisis. By 1899, the *Estates Gazette* could observe: 'This country appears to care little for the position of land . . . Unquestionably, politicians mould their conduct on the wishes of the towns rather than on the country.' Meanwhile, Lord Ernle, in his *English Farming*, wrote:

> The legislature was powerless to provide any substantial help. Food was, so to speak, the currency in which foreign nations paid for English manufactured goods, and its cheapness was an undoubted blessing to the wage-earning

community. Thrown on their own resources, agriculturalists fought the unequal contest with courage and tenacity. But as time went on, the stress told more and more heavily. Manufacturing populations seemed to seek food markets everywhere except at home. Enterprise gradually weakened; landlords lost their ability to help, farmers their recuperative powers. Prolonged depression checked costly improvements. Drainage was practically discontinued. Both owners and occupiers were engaged in the task of making both ends meet on vanishing incomes. Land deteriorated in condition; less labour was employed; less stock was kept; bills for cake and fertilisers were reduced. The counties which suffered most were the corn-growing districts in which high farming had won its most signal triumphs.

Initially the depression was restricted to the corn-growing areas of the UK: by 1900 the acreage under corn had dropped from eight million acres to six million, a fall of some twenty-five per cent. However, livestock farmers did not escape for long as during the 1890s ships began arriving with frozen meat from the colonies, thus causing even this sector to be plunged into recession.

This was not, of course, the first agricultural depression. As we have seen farming had suffered before, most recently at the end of the Napoleonic Wars between 1815 and 1824, but unlike previous recessions in the farming industry this one was to last a very long time indeed.

It seemed the attack on land was not to be limited to a collapse in food prices. From out of the valleys of Wales came a man with a silver tongue and a loathing for landowners – Lloyd George; he was to wage a long running war on landowners until the advent of the First World War diverted his energies to other avenues.

It was a Conservative government that, bowing to pressure from the middle classes about a so-called monopoly of land, commissioned what is sometimes called 'the New Domesday' but was officially called *A Return of Owners of Land*. It was compiled between 1874 and 1876, and although the operation was incompetently carried out – in stark contrast to William the

Conqueror's effort some eight hundred years previously – it was to provide much ammunition to the increasingly vocal anti-landowner lobby. It found that 25% of the British Isles was owned by 1,200 people while 66.14% of the total land area was owned by 10,911 people, who individually owned land in excess of a thousand acres each. Naturally this percentage varied considerably over the country. In Scotland, for instance the percentage held by landowners was over 92%, while in England it was only 56%. It is interesting to note that in France, at about the same time, there were only around a thousand estates with more than a thousand acres, such had been the ravages of revolution and the Code Napoléon.

These returns were published in four large volumes which an enterprising gentleman called John Bateman edited, producing an invaluable reference work called *The Great Landowners of Great Britain and Ireland*. His book concentrated on those landowners with three thousand acres or more who were in receipt of an income of three thousand plus, however he did deign to include details of some estates and incomes which fell just below this category.

It was then as common a misapprehension, among the mass of the public, as it is today that a landowner is rich. To a true landowner, of course, the value of his property is only of an interest when he is speaking to his bank manager. Otherwise it is an irritant. Foolish people talk in terms of so and so being worth millions because he happens to own two thousand acres of land, and technically this is the case, but he is only as rich as his net income until he sells his land, and as the true landowner has no intention of doing this he does not regard himself as rich. Bateman tackled this subject by drawing up an imaginary annual profit-and-loss account for a squire with a 3,500 acre estate and a income of £5,000. He called his typical £5,000-a-year squire John Steadyman, of Wearywork Hall, Cidershire.

INCOME FROM RENTS	£5000
Deduct for value in the rate books put upon mansion, grounds, etc.	£220
Deduct also value put on cottages lived in rent free by old retainers	£30
Leaving a clear rent roll of	**£4,750**
EXPENSES – now deduct as under –	
His late fathers two maiden sisters, Jane & Esther, who each have a rent charge of £180 per annum (n.b. both these old ladies seem immortal)	£360
His mother, Lady Louisa Steadyman, a rent charge of	£700
His sisters, Louisa, Marian and Eve (all plain), each £150	£450
His brother, Wildbore Steadyman, was paid off but almost always comes down annually for say	£50
Mortgage on Sloppyside Farm & Hungry Hill (from when his father contested the county) interest	£650
Mortgage on Wearywork End (started when his one pretty sister married and was paid off)	£150
His estate agent, Mr Harrable, salary	£150
Keep of horse for Mr Harrable	£35
House for Mr Harrable	£45
Lawyers' bills	£60
Farm repairs	£350
Draining tiles given free to tenants	£40
Repairs to mansion house	£70
Voluntary church rate, pensions, local charities, etc.	£175
Subscription to political party	£10
Subscription to the Cidershire Foxhounds & Boggymoor Harriers	£30
Subscription to the Diocesan	£25
Other county subscriptions – hospitals, races, etc.	£35
Returned 15% of rents in 'hard times', averaging perhaps one year in five (would that we could say so now in 1882)	£150
Loss on occasional bankrupt tenants	£30
Arreas of rent, say annually, £300; loss of interest thereon @ 5%	£15
Income tax at 4d in the pound on rents paid and unpaid	£83
Insurance on all buildings	£55
TOTAL OUTGOINGS	£3,718

This left our worthy squire the magnificent annual sum of £1,032 to live on.

Actually if we multiply poor Mr Steadyman's net income of £1,032 by say a factor of 100 to allow for inflation he doesn't, to our eyes, seem quite as badly off as Mr Bateman makes out. A clear income of over £100,000 after tax and expenses is not to be sneezed at and I very much doubt if many 3,500-acre estates could boast one as big today.

Of course, Bateman was writing at the time when the great agricultural depression was only just beginning to bite. Over the next fifty years landowners' net disposable incomes were to plummet by up to 90%, as a glance at the table below will show.

Average gross rent per acre		
1872	1938	1946
34s. 6d.	25s. 6d.	27s. 6d.

So between 1872 and 1946 gross rents fell by some 25%, but that of course is only part of the story. Mr Bateman's Squire Steadyman paid only 4d in the pound or less than 2% of his gross income in income tax. His descendant in 1946 would have paid more like 80% on his net income. At the same time wages for workers, such as gardeners, gamekeepers, building workers, foresters and domestic servants, had increased enormously. In 1873 the average farmworker in England received 13s. a week, by 1914 this had risen to 25s. a week and by 1920 it peaked at 42s. a week, before falling back as farming went back into recession. By 1948, though wages for farmworkers had reached £5 a week, the gross income of landowners had remained static and their outgoings in the form of staff wages had multiplied alarmingly. To add to their woes, few of the estate tasks had yet been mechanised – for instance, gamekeepers, foresters, gardeners, carpenters, masons and the like still worked in virtually the same manner as their grandfathers had done in the nineteenth century. The industrial revolution had, as yet, hardly encroached at all on the working practices of the average estate workforce.

Rents, in fact, did not begin to exceed the 1870 levels in nominal terms till the late 1960s! and only now – in 1998 – are they remotely comparable to 1870, when the ravages of inflation are taken into account.

Looking at such figures it is hardly to be wondered at that so many landowners elected to call it a day and sell up between 1910 and 1979. The wonder is that there are any decent sized estates left at all! That there are can be put down to a number of reasons.

Some large landowners of course were the descendants of those *parvenus* businessmen of the late nineteenth century who had kept their business empire together and were thus able to continue to subsidise their country estate out of business profits. Other landowners had such a large acreage to start with that they were able to carry out a long-term policy of selling outlying areas to raise capital to pay for running expenses, without destroying the heart of their estate. There were a few landowners lucky in having sizeable chunks of urban property, and others could sell off works of art.

The ones who suffered most were, of course, Bateman's Squire Steadyman and his ilk. They did not have the advantages of their noble kinsmen's vast acreages or valuable art collections or urban property portfolios and had always relied totally on the income from their estate. For them Armageddon beckoned. That any survived at all was a minor miracle, due in the main to that old-fashioned virtue we have mentioned before, guts –the refusal to surrender, the determination to survive.

During the First World War, the government, alarmed by the success of the U-boat campaign and anxious to encourage the expansion of the wheat acreage, brought in the 1917 Corn Protection Act; this act enabled – for a short period – bumper profits to be made by tenant farmers, though little of this prosperity filtered up to the landowner. In 1921, the Corn Protection Act was abolished and farmers and landowners were once again at the mercy of free world prices; wheat prices almost immediately dropped by 50%; by 1931 wheat had fallen to 24s. 8d. a quarter – the lowest price recorded (except for a brief period in 1894–5) in a history of agricultural statistics

going back as far as 1780! As at this time the cost of growing
and harvesting an acre of wheat was estimated at around £8 an
acre (compared with an average today of around £240 per acre),
average yields being about 30 hundredweight, it can be seen that
farming in the 1930s was indeed *in extremis.* The government
finally woke up to the disaster and in 1932 brought in the Wheat
Act which effectively marked the end of an era. Except for the
brief period of 1917–21, for almost a hundred years, from the
abolition of the Corn Laws in 1846 to 1932, British agriculture
had survived, and at times prospered, without any form of
protection from free world markets.

The Wheat Act was the beginning of the British system of
subsidising farming which goes by the name of deficiency
payments and was, together with marketing boards for specific
products, to provide the template for all forms of UK
subsidisation until Britain entered the Common Market.
Interestingly, one of the reasons why the general public was
willing to accept some form of agricultural protection in the
1930s was that food from retailing outlets no longer reflected
the cost of the basic raw material; for instance, between 1924
and 1931 the price of wheat halved, yet a loaf of bread only fell
from 8*d.* to 7*d.* over the same time.

In short, the Wheat Act forced all farmers to register their
wheat acreage and guaranteed them a price of 45*s.* a quarter (the
average cost of production being estimated at 40*s.* a quarter).
The farmer was to be paid the difference between the average
price of home-grown wheat and the price for which the miller
could have bought the wheat on the world market (the
'deficiency' price) on all wheat of a millable quality delivered to
the miller. In order to protect itself from farmers switching into
wheat in large numbers, however, the government set a ceiling
on the amount of wheat it would pay out on at six million
quarters.

So the period between the wars was a very rough one for both
farmers and landowners. It was an especially tough time for
those farmers who, encouraged by the large profits they had
made during the First War, had borrowed money and bought
their own farms from landowners eager to sell in the immediate

aftermath of the war. Although landowners also suffered during this depression, at least they weren't subjected to the various forms of land nationalisation and expropriation which, after 1918, were inflicted on most continental landowners. The new countries carved out of the carcasses of the old German Reich, the Austro-Hungarian Empire and the Russian Empire embarked on an orgy of land reform aimed at reducing or eliminating large private estates and filling up the land with 'smallholders'. In Romania individual ownership of more than a hundred hectares in mountain districts and two hundred hectares elsewhere was forbidden. In Czechoslovakia about one third of the total land area changed hands, while in Estonia all the properties of the great landowners were seized. In Poland expropriation and subdivision were initially limited to the land of specific owners, such as the church and members of the previous reigning families, and all land which was 'badly managed', but ultimately all private ownership of more than four hundred hectares of land became outlawed. Similar stories could be told of virtually every country in Europe. Not that there was not much talk of carrying out a similar programme in the UK; there was, but it never happened. The consequences of this massive pan-European agricultural revolution are still with us today, although of course the aftermath of the Second World War brought about the 'collectivisation' of many of these small-holdings in Eastern Europe.

But 1946 was to be a watershed in the decline of agriculture in Britain. The country was still in the grip of rationing and the main aim of the government was to boost home food production to try and narrow the import gap. The policy chosen was to be a mixture of improvement grants and price support. The twin aims were cheap food for the masses and a healthy farming economy, saving precious foreign exchange by producing at home what we had previously imported from abroad.

It is ironic that, when we look at newspaper coverage of agriculture today, we often read of our farmers being castigated for carrying out a policy which only a generation ago they were being urged to follow. It may be of some comfort to the farming community to realise that this is a characteristic British reaction to success. Anyone who has ever served in the armed forces is well aware of it; as Kipling wrote so perceptively:

> For it's Tommy this, an' Tommy that, an', 'Chuck him
> out, the brute!'
> But it's 'Saviour of 'is country' when the guns begin
> to shoot.

A typical example of the sort of press comment which farmers today have to put up with is this extract from an article in the *Daily Mail* by the highly respected columnist Andrew Alexander, on 20 January 1998:

> If there is one body of men to whom we should not entrust the care of the countryside, it is the farmers. Their record over the past fifty years or so has been appalling. If they see a hedgerow they want to uproot it. If they have trees in their fields, especially mature trees with sizeable roots, they want to cut them down. If it were not for shooting and the woodland required for it the countryside would have been even more desolated.

Of course, in the dash for modernisation and increased production mistakes were made – no one would deny that. Some land was brought into production at a totally unacceptable cost – both economically and environmentally – but back in the late forties and early fifties cost was not an issue and the word 'environment' had yet to feature in our everyday language – feeding the population and saving foreign exchange was the name of the game. A good example of wrong thinking during this period was the wholesale grant-funded drainage schemes carried out throughout the country on wetlands. The end result has been disastrous, not only for the environment but also in purely economic terms. Drainage schemes on wetlands meant that rain, instead of soaking into the natural sponge of the soil, ran off at once into rivers. Towns and villages which had never known floods in history now found themselves on the receiving end of them, and hundreds of millions of pounds had to be spent on flood defences. At the same time, rivers which had once been fed by the water seeping gently out of the wetlands over a long period became discoloured spate rivers, carrying tons of silt down to the estuaries; valuable Salmon rivers were wrecked.

Conservationists and the like should not despair, however, about many of the 'improvements' carried out by farmers over the last fifty years. Most are easily reversible and many of the bogs and marginal land drained in the last fifty years will in all probability revert to their old state as farming on such terrain ceases to be profitable. Indeed, any person who cares to take a spade into a field and dig a trench will discover that over the last few hundred years generation after generation of farmers have had a crack at draining a field during the good times, only to let it go back when the bad times come.

The vast dispersal of so much land since 1910 has, of course, fundamentally altered the English countryside. The removal of land from the ownership of a small group of, on the whole, benign landowners, who took pride in their ancestral acres, and their replacement by men who, on the whole, viewed land as purely a means of making money has caused much of the damage to the English landscape which people bemoan today. It is one of the ironies of life that those who complain most about factory farming, the proliferation of unsightly developments, the despoiling of our villages are, more often than not, the same people who raise a glass of elderflower champagne to their lips to toast the demise of yet another old family that has been forced finally to sell the family estate.

For it is a truism that if you admire a piece of unspoilt landscape or a village not ruined by unsympathetic development, nine times out of ten you will find it is either owned by a private estate, or once was and is now owned by the National Trust.

The horrors of taxation, and especially the taxation bias against what was deemed to be unearned income, resulted in many landowners deciding, during the late fifties and early sixties, that to survive they must get their hands dirty and work. Looking around in a desultory fashion at the opportunities open to them, many latched on to the natural choice of farming. Farming his own land had numerous attractions for a land-owner, so when a tenant died or retired landowners started 'taking the land back in hand'.

Initially this worked well. The tax regime was not geared to cater for farmers who had other sources of income beside their in-hand farms and landowners discovered to their delight that they were on a heads-I-win-tales-you-lose scenario as far as the taxman was concerned. Losses on the home farm could be set off against other income, so even if they were to lose money the taxman effectively gave them back over ninety per cent of their losses, while if they made money they paid tax at an earned-income rate.

No one, of course, likes losing money, even if someone else picks up ninety per cent of the losses, but landowners discovered that many expenses could be put through the farm account which, while technically allowable against tax, had in the old days been paid out of net income. Gardeners and gamekeepers, for instance, metamorphosed into farmworkers, drives became farm roads and were done up accordingly, cars became farm vehicles, and so on; the end result was very favourable to the landowner who took land in hand.

This happy turn of events lasted till the late sixties when an unsporting Labour government insisted that farms should show a profit at least once every five years to justify the tax advantages. However, this proved not to be too arduous for all but the least efficient home farms – although there were quite a large number of these, many of whose owners found, to their surprise, that it was more difficult than they thought to make money out of farming. The reason for this gradually dawned on them – though it is fair to say it still has not dawned on everyone – that gentlemen make bad farmers. Many gentlemen had already taken this fact on board and had effectively subcontracted their farming to a character called a farm manager. The problem with this approach was at once apparent – the farm manager needed to be paid. If the home farm was not of sufficient size all the profits went to pay the farm manager's salary. Even if there were excess profits in the odd year, landowners found the farm manager always had a good idea of how to spend them, so very little ready cash ever seemed to end up in their pockets. In short, they had forgotten, if they had ever been taught, the ditty:

> He who by the plough would thrive,
> Himself must either hold or drive.

However, the biased tax treatment on earned as opposed to unearned income was such that landowners who had become involved in farming eagerly took every farm in hand when it became vacant – it was, in short, the only way they could see to survive. Perhaps they also believed what their farm managers and professional advisers told then *ad infinitum,* namely that the larger the farm the greater the profits would be due to a mysterious thing called 'economies of scale'. The end result has been that the percentage of land farmed by tenants has continued to fall inexorably and is now hovering just above twenty per cent of the total agricultural acreage in the country – down from over ninety per cent in 1900.

The arrival of Mrs Thatcher in No. 10 Downing Street heralded a dramatic change in taxation policies. As the rate of tax fell and the bias against unearned income disappeared, suddenly making farming losses became rather less attractive. When the marginal rate of tax is over ninety per cent frankly losing a few thousand is no big deal, but when it falls to forty per cent even the stupidest landowner can see that there is a problem.

Future agricultural historians will look on the years of the Conservative government, 1979–97, as one of the boom times in agriculture; this – it is true – owed much to the entry of the UK into the Common Market and the Common Agricultural Policy (CAP), of which more later, but it also saw the emergence of a new creature on the agricultural scene – the contract farmer.

Landowners with loss-making farms had a problem. What to do with them? They were loath to relet them – partly perhaps from pride, but also because although income-tax differentials between earned and unearned income had disappeared there was still a substantial bias against let land in the form of capital taxes, namely death duties. Also reletting would mean putting a tenant in, and since 1976, due to what can probably be described as one of the stupidest bills ever passed by Parliament, tenants had been given the right to pass their farm on to their son. This bill, proudly backed by the National Farmers Union (NFU) – the leadership of which is not particularly well known for having large reserves of grey matter at the best of times, but in this instance conclusively proved it was entirely vacant in the top storey – effectively managed, at a stroke, totally to destroy the market in new farms for tenants, thus adding greater impetus to the formation of larger and larger farming units and making it virtually impossible for young men of limited means to get into farming on their own account.

Fortunately for landowners there was a solution at hand – contract farming. This was the brainchild of lawyers and land agents working together over the years to develop a way by which landowners could effectively 'let' their farm without granting an agricultural tenancy; in other words, it gave land-owners many of the benefits of tenanted land with none of the downside.

Thus a contract farmer enters into what is effectively a partnership agreement with the landowner. In return for the landowner providing the capital – in the form of land – the contract farmer guarantees to pay him a fixed sum – called the rent equivalent – of, say £80 per acre, and also a share of the profits. Hurray – for the landowner a truly blissful arrangement! – he gets all the advantages of having a tenant yet none of the hassle. His contract is for a set period of years; he gets a regular income; he keeps his working-farmer status for purposes of taxation; he gets a decent slice of the action when profits are good; and he does not have to worry about tenants' rights and all the other minor problems that bedevil the average land-owner, or wonder, if he is farming in hand, by how much his farm manager is ripping him off.

The contractor benefits enormously as well. He can achieve huge economies of scale, which, with farm machinery getting bigger and more expensive, he needs, and because usually he is genuinely an extremely efficient farmer, he will produce handsome profits not only for himself but for the landowner.

The end result has been yet another radical alteration in the British countryside. Houses once lived in by tenant farmers are now redundant and are sold off to weekenders or, if near enough to big cities, executives of banks and the like who commute into work. The number of jobs on the land plummet as the contractor achieves the promised economies of scale which allow him to pay the landowner his 'rent equivalent' and share of the profits. As a rough rule of thumb, a fifteen-hundred-acre arable farm might give a living to two families – the owner and a farmworker. At the other end of the scale, that same fifteen hundred acres could today support up to five tenant farms, each probably providing a livelihood for on average one and half families – perhaps more in a livestock-farming area. It is ironic that one of the primary reasons for the demise of the tenant farmer can be laid at the feet of the one organisation which was supposed to represent him – the NFU!

But then, sadly, the NFU has often exhibited all the faults associated with traditional trade unionism in the UK in being over-concerned about achieving short-term benefits for existing members rather than acting for the long-term health of the industry. Such 'short-term' attitudes, combined with a fear of offending any farming member, have undoubtedly contributed to the fall from grace of the farming industry in the eyes of the general public over the last thirty years.

It is fair to say, however, that the NFU has at last woken up to the stupidity of its old policy and has given its support to a new form of tenancy called a Farm Business Tenancy; this allows a landlord to let his farm on whatever terms can be agreed between himself and a willing tenant. The result has been that a little more land has been made available for letting – but its probable effect will not be to raise the level of land at present farmed by tenants to much above its present level, but rather to act as a brake on the total demise of the tenanted sector. Interestingly the much vaunted Farm Business Tenancy is virtually identical in form to the tenancy agreements devised by our Tudor ancestors in the late sixteenth century. So much for progress.

I suppose it is yet another minor miracle of the British countryside that any tenant farmers still exist at all, bearing in mind the best efforts of successive governments and the NFU to destroy the sector. Many commentators would argue that their continued existence is down to idle and unenterprising landowners. It is an argument which I find difficult to refute. Certainly no commercially run business would have tolerated the continuation of tenants, especially when the value of the attractive farmhouses in which they live rent free escalated through the roof back in the 1980s. And yet many landowners, to the amazement of most people, continue to take a rather less than commercial view of their estates and relet farms as and when they become vacant. Perhaps they see their estate as not so much a vehicle to be driven to its economic limits but rather one to be nurtured and allowed – providing it will still get you from A to B – to chug along quietly in the slow lane.

However, even the owner of the most traditionally run estate has since the war been amalgamating holdings and investing in new farm buildings on his tenanted farms. For the sad fact is that small tenanted farms are uneconomic for a landowner. To understand this it is necessary to remember that – to all intents and purposes – the tenant lives rent free in the farmhouse. Imagine two farms of a hundred acres each, both equipped with a nice spacious traditional farmhouse. Both are paying a rent of £50 per acre or £5,000 a year each. Then one gives up; the landowner amalgamates the two farms and, in this simplified model, still gets £50 per acre rent for the two hundred acres but now lets the redundant farmhouse on an assured shorthold tenancy for £5,000 per year. In other words the landowner has increased his rent by fifty per cent.

Actually it is arguable whether a tenant or farmer needs any longer to live on a farm. Many tenants themselves rent additional land 'off farm', for which they are often – strangely – prepared to pay a far higher rent than for the land in the immediate vicinity of their farmhouse. We shall have to see how the letting of land under the New Farm Business Tenancy Act develops, but my guess is that landowners are going to be less and less likely to 'chuck in the house for nothing' when discussing rental terms with prospective tenants.

Not that the tenant system could have been dismantled overnight anyway, even if landowners had wished it. Tenant farmers, depending at what date they took up their tenancy,

have many legal rights, not least, in the case of those with pre-
1976 tenancies, of inheritance.

Of course, the changes which have taken place have not gone
unnoticed by commentators in land-management techniques and
forms of tenure, and contract farmers and the like are in receipt
of considerable flack from environmentalists and conservationists everywhere. There is much talk of moving back to
'sustainable' farming, by which, ironically, they mean the
opposite of what they say. For farming has done what for
generations people demanded – provided ever cheaper food for
the urban masses. A ton of wheat in 1996 sold for between £90
and £120 per ton; back in 1881 it sold for £10.65 a ton. In modern
money that is over £700 per ton. If that is not sustainable
farming, I don't know what is. One vaguely wonders what some of
today's critics of farming would have to say if the price of wheat
had kept pace with inflation and was now around £700 a ton! I
suspect they might find their weekly shopping expedition to
Sainsbury's a rather bigger financial burden than it is at present.

In fact, of course, they would be urging that every last square
foot of land to be brought into production. For it is only because
farming today worldwide is so efficient that the urban population
can give rein to their conservationist instincts. If the price of
wheat were ever to rise significantly, the knock-on effect on the
price of food in the shops would cause an uproar. In other words,
low food prices caused by efficient food production are good for
conservation.

It is true to say, however, that the farming industry as it is
presently run and financed is not sustainable in the long term.
No industry which produces more than there is demand to
satisfy can long continue to operate in the same way – this is
commonsense. The problem with food production is a simple
one – there is only so much food you can cram into your tummy
during a day; *ergo* constant increases in production by farmers
need to be matched by increases in population, i.e. market. With
the population of Europe showing no sign of expanding, we need
new markets to sell the surplus to if the farming industry is to
remain 'sustainable'; or we need profits, and therefore land
prices, to fall to such a level that large areas of farmland are

taken out of production because they are uneconomic and put to some other profitable use. This does not necessarily mean these areas have to be taken out of farming *per se;* it could mean that farmland which has been intensively farmed reverts to being extensively farmed so that production per acre falls. This is, in fact, exactly what happened during the great agricultural depression – the corn acreage shrank by around forty per cent as marginal corn-growing land reverted to grassland.

There is one inescapable fact which our short overview of the history of land ownership has confirmed. Landowning has always been about money. There appears to be some vague idea buried in the minds of many of those who pontificate on the environment that past owners of land somehow did not bother about the sordid subject of making cash but were happy to live in a sort of Arcadian society were country gentlemen in palatial seats co-existed with happy and contented peasantry, milking a few cows.

The desire of landowners to manage their land for maximum efficiency and to improve their estates is not new but as old as civilisation and – contrary to what the environmentalist would have you believe – there is not one acre of land in the United Kingdom that has not been affected by man's desire to extract money from the earth. We have already seen from entries in the Domesday Book of 1086 that our Norman ancestors were very competent improvers. Agricultural improvement is like a craze, throughout history it goes in and out of fashion. For instance, the late sixteenth and early seventeenth centuries were a period of great agricultural improvement. It was a time when landowners started to drain the fens and marshes and enclose land. To this, it is fair to say, there was strenuous opposition from those who feared the resulting efficiencies would cause widespread depopulation and hardship in rural areas – which of course is what they did. Periods of improvement tend to coincide with times when the price of agricultural produce is high and landowners' expenditure is rising, causing them to look at barren and unproductive acres with a gleam in their eye and wonder how to bring that land into production.

Not that every farmer and landowner in history has been an 'improver'. Improving land is capital intensive and the profits are in the future while the costs are borne today. Many landowners, both past and present, would sympathise with the view of the eighteenth-century academic who was being urged to spend money on improving college lands for posterity and retorted: 'We are always talking of doing for posterity, I would fain see posterity do something for us.'

But then farmers and landowners are no different from any other businessmen. There are the conservative ones, husbanding scarce resources, and the risk-takers, borrowing money, expanding, modernising and dreaming not of survival but of enormous riches in the future. Since the war, of course, the industrial sector of the UK has changed radically. We might bemoan the standardisation of the high streets of our market towns by chains of building societies and chemists and the concerted and continuing attack made on small grocers, butchers and the like by 'out of town' monster supermarkets, but, like it or loathe it, it is progress of a sort, and leads to cheaper food and other products for the sainted consumer. Farming is no different. Like other businesses, it benefits from economies of scale and, like other businesses, the people who run it are fighting in a competitive world to survive.

The chief cause for criticism of farming is that, over the last fifty years, its modernisation has been funded by enormous taxpayers' subsidies in one form or another. The universal assumption seems to be that without such dollops of public money being spent on it we would today have a very different farming industry, and one more in keeping with what the 'public' would like to see.

In one way this view is correct – we would have a very different farming industry. History teaches us that low prices and tight margins in any industry encourage amalgamations and suchlike. In other words, a Britain without a subsidised farming sector would probably be a Britain with even fewer farmers than at present and an even more 'industrialised' farming sector. If you doubt this diagnosis look at what has happened to the retail sector since the abolition in 1964 of Retail Price Maintenance.

Subsidies for all their faults (which are many) have acted as a brake on the 'industrialisation' of farming – not as a spur, as they are often represented as having done. Nevertheless the trend towards larger farms is one which is set to continue. In 1950 Britain had some 550,000 farmers who employed around one million farmworkers; today there are only some 220,000 farmers, ten per cent of whom produce some fifty per cent of the total food consumption of the country. These figures may horrify some, but my guess is that without the cushion of subsidies the number of UK farmers would have fallen by a much greater amount.

The provision of subsidies has been seized upon in their arguments by certain pressure groups; the Ramblers, for instance, see it as a justification for their demand for 'public access' or the 'right to roam'. They argue that because farmers have been in receipt of so much public money in the form of subsidies then the taxpayer should have the 'right' to walk over the land. This argument is patently flawed. Few industries have not been in receipt of some form of government subsidy over the years – the railways, the car industry, the steel industry, ship-building, electronics, aerospace, textiles, tourism, all have had their fair share of handouts, and many of these subsidies are still running today. The railways still get a large annual sum, as does virtually every major factory investment. If every business which had ever received a government subsidy was, retrospectively, forced to provide public access, then there would not be one square foot of the United Kingdom from which walkers could be excluded. For instance, many of the Ramblers probably live in houses which they have bought with mortgages subsidised via Mortgage Interest Tax Relief, or have had their roofs insulated with the help of a grant. So, taking their argument to its logical conclusion, this fact would allow anybody to walk in and inspect every nook and cranny of their property whenever they felt like it. Also it would be grossly unfair and inequitable to alter the conditions of grants and subsidies retrospectively. It could be argued, though, that if the government ever wanted to, it could make grants and subsidies in the future conditional on public access – and, indeed there are schemes, such as Country Stewardship, where this is actually the case.

Contrary to the opinion of many conservationists, not all farm improvements are bad for wildlife. It is one of the ironies of country life that yesterday's farm improvement is all too often today's wildlife habitat. No more classic example exists of this than that of hedgerows. Recently an Act of Parliament was passed to protect hedgerows. It is worth recalling, however, that the majority of them are of comparatively recent origin. The great age of enclosures was the nineteenth century. Prior to 1845 enclosures required a special Act of Parliament which was extremely expensive. The Enclosure Acts of 1801 and 1836 simplified the procedure but it was not until 1845 that the requirement for an Act of Parliament before enclosing land was finally abolished. Up till that date most of the land in the Midlands was virtually open country. Hedgerows were then planted as agricultural improvements, now they are protected as wildlife habitats.

Of course, some parts of England were enclosed much earlier. Of Devon, J. A. Venn, in *The Foundations of Agricultural Economics* (1933), wrote:

> The average field is some four or five acres in extent, instead of ten or twenty found elsewhere in England, and there is no doubt that such parcels of land form serious obstacles to efficient arable farming. Calculations have been made that show the direct loss of space from excessively wide banks and hedges alone amounts to some 6% of the farming area, and, if the further loss caused by shade is included, this figure may be increased to anything from 10%–20%. Added to this is the handicap entailed by use . . . of abnormally small instruments, and the sheer inability to introduce certain types of machinery into them . . .

In view of this, it is little to be wondered at that so many hedgerows were removed – once again the wonder is that so many were not. Today I suspect more hedgerows are being planted than are being grubbed up. But sadly no one seems very interested in this good news. This is not surprising, as we all know that good news does not sell newspapers and it is far more fun – for a journalist – to announce, in banner headlines, 'farmers grub up two thousand miles of hedgerows a year' – even though such figures are not based on anything other than guesswork. Actually, even if the figure of two thousand miles were correct – which it isn't – it is not a very large amount in the scheme of things. For example, on my own three-thousand acre estate I have over one hundred miles of hedgerow and woodland edge, and three thousand acres is less than five square miles of land.

But the point everyone should remember is that from the most barren Scottish hillside to the seemingly unspoilt downs of Southern England, all stand witness to man's efforts to make money out of them. There is no wood or stream or hill in this country of ours which has not been worked for profit at some time in its history. The ignorant who bemoan modern farming and forestry methods forget, conveniently, that at one time the Highlands of Scotland were covered in trees and that England was devoid of hedgerows. Today, of course, landowners are castigated both for planting trees on hillsides and for removing hedgerows, when they could logically argue that by so doing they were returning the land to a similar state in which it existed in, say, the tenth century.

CHAPTER 7

Scotland

Land of brown heather and shaggy wood.
SIR WALTER SCOTT

Scotland, as the Scots never stop telling us Englishmen, is different from the rest of the British Isles – and how right they are. Soon it will be even more different, when the Scottish Parliament is finally ensconced in luxury in Edinburgh, and the betting must be that within the next twenty years Scotland will, to all intents and purposes, revert to its status prior to the Act of Union of 1709. It may surprise most Scotsmen that a large number of Englishmen can't wait for that happy state of affairs to be accomplished.

Before we look at the modern rural economy of Highland estates it is well to take a quick overview of Scottish landed history since the Act of Union in 1709, especially as there can be few countries where the role of myth and legend is as important in the thinking of the inhabitants today as it was in the past.

In 1709, rural Scotland was still being run on feudal lines with the Scottish Parliament dominated by the great nobles. Poor tenants held their land from the lairds on annually terminable leases and hence had little incentive to improve their farms, while the lairds themselves were, by comparison with their English equivalents, poor – a landowner with a rent roll of five hundred pounds a year was considered a very rich man indeed – and had little spare cash to invest in their estates. In short, rural Scotland in 1709 had progressed little since the middle ages.

Romantics in Scotland have always regretted the Act of Union but they forget the harshness of contemporary conditions: only a short time prior to the Union there had been a period of six consecutive disastrous harvests (1694–1700) when famine had struck rural Scotland and many tens of thousands of people had died of starvation. It is true that since then there had been some good harvests but the memory of the dark days at the end of seventeenth century, when Scotland had no money to import wheat and its citizens died in droves from hunger, must have been uppermost in the minds of many in 1709.

At the same time Highland Scotland was still a tribal society, depending for its livelihood on selling cattle to the Lowlanders in exchange for corn, and carrying out the odd raid on them when they felt the urge.

One of the great myths of Scotland is that the large Highland estates were once 'tribal' lands and that it was only after the '45 rebellion that the wicked chiefs appropriated the land for themselves. This is simply not true; even before the '45, Highland crofters who wanted land to farm had always had to hire it from the 'tacksman' who in turn had leased the ground from the chief.

Once the Act of Union was passed Scottish agriculture began a century of improvement. At first, go-ahead lairds imported English ploughmen and farmers to teach their tenants the new ways, but such was the Scottish farmer's aptitude for taking on board and then himself improving on the new ideas that by the end of century it was Scottish ploughmen and stewards who were heading south to pass on their knowledge to Englishmen!

The old annual tenancies were terminated and new larger and more efficient farms were carved out of the land and let on long leases of nineteen years or more; fields were enclosed, drained, limed and manured as, with a longer period of tenure, tenants now had an incentive to improve their land.

As for the Highlands, the end of the '45 rebellion brought new roads, built by General Wade, and this meant that for the first time in history the Highlands of Scotland became part of the mainstream of Scottish life. Because of this the chiefs lost most of their old feudal power over their tribesmen and began to change into traditional landowners. In short, the 'civilisation' of the Highlands had begun. As with the civilisation of any warlike people this was to lead to hardship, since the banding together of families and men under the protection of a strong chief, who could, and did, defend them from attacks by adjacent clans and, on occasions, led them in raids on their Lowland neighbours, had been one of the *raisons d'être* of the clan system. Once the rule of law was established, the claymore had to be put aside and the warrior ethos of clan life was gone. It is one of the great ironies that those who most deplore the collapse of the 'noble savage', be it Zulu or Highlander, fail to realise that it is the inexorable march of civilisation and their own unwillingness to put up with old-fashioned rape and pillage which have brought about the demoralisation and collapse of a tribal system which they purport to admire.

By the start of the nineteenth century the Lowland lairds and their tenants were enjoying a prosperity which their ancestors would surely never have dreamt possible, but in the Highlands the 'clearances' (1785–1850) had already begun. This sad but inevitable page in Scottish history was dictated by economic and demographic necessity. The population in the Highlands was rising and, as a result, farms were getting smaller as they were divided up among an increasing population living in poverty. It is true that the economic motive behind many of the clearances was the profitability of sheep, but a large-scale migration from the glens would have occurred sooner or later. It is hardly likely that Highlanders would have been content to remain living in poverty when the Industrial Revolution arrived and jobs in the booming metropolis of Glasgow became available. It could also be argued that the clearances prevented a far greater tragedy occurring. The Highland farmer, like his Irish cousin, had begun to rely on the potato, and so the potato blight which caused the Irish famine of 1847–51 had a similar effect on the remaining crofters. It is less the fact of the clearances than the manner in which they were carried out by some landowners – notably the Duke of Sutherland – which has caused them to rankle ever since in the minds of many Scotsmen.

The beginning of the Englishman's unrequited love affair with Scotland was the triumphant visit of George IV to Edinburgh, so ably orchestrated by Sir Walter Scott; conjuring myth and legend into fact, he squeezed the fat German into flesh-coloured tights and a Highland costume of his own design. With his novels, which became required reading for the rapidly expanding middle classes of Scotland and England, it was Sir Walter Scott who began the romanticisation of Scotland and all things Scottish. The public imagination was still further stirred by the paintings of Sir Edwin Landseer, and no Victorian parlour was complete without its print of the *Monarch of the Glen*. On a series of visits north of the border, Queen Victoria herself fell in love with the Highlands and in 1848 purchased Balmoral, not such an impractical step now that the new railways, thrusting deep into the very heart of the region, made the dream accessible to all.

Even so, by 1880 the concept of rich Englishmen buying a Scottish sporting estate was still a long way off. In 1880 it was calculated that 1,741 Scots landowners held more than a 1,000 acres each and owned 92% of the country. The descendants of the old Highland chiefs often had massive holdings in acreage terms, although it has to be said that the land area was rarely reflected in the income generated.

Owner	Acres	Gross annual value
Duke of Sutherland	1,325,453	£68,939
Earl of Breadalbane	438,358	£58,292
Duke of Buccleuch	432,927	£172,929
Sir Charles Ross Bt	356,500	£17,264
Earl of Seafield	305,930	£78,227
Duke of Richmond & Gordon	269,294	£60,400
Earl of Fife	249,220	£72,563
Duke of Athole	201,640	£42,030
Duke of Argyll	175,114	£50,842
Sir Kenneth Mackenzie Bt	164,680	£9,344

Source: Bateman's *Great Landowners of Great Britain and Ireland*

The top ten landowners in Scotland in 1880 are listed above. The picture today is very different. (I am aware that many of these estates are not 'owned' in the true sense of the word by

Owner	Acres
Forestry Commission	1,600,000
Duke of Buccleuch	270,000
Scottish Office -Agriculture Department	260,000
National Trust for Scotland	190,000
Alcan Highland Estates	135,000
Duke of Atholl	130,000
Captain Farquharson	125,000
Duchess of Westminster	120,000
Earl of Seafield	105,000
Crown Estates	100,000

Source: *Who Owns Scotland Now?* by Ausian Cramb, 1996

the people named but are often held in forms of trust.)

A glance will demonstrate that since 1880 there has been in Scotland, as in England, a vast sell-off by traditional owners. The result is that now over 2,456,000 acres are held by either state bodies, charities (such as the RSPB, which owns 87,400 acres) or public companies, such as Alcan. This is over 12% of the total land area of Scotland.

It must have been a source of great joy to the average Highland landowner, saddled with an enormous estate which yielded only a pittance in income, when he discovered that rich English and Scottish industrialists dreamed of owning a small part of his domain and were willing to pay him good money to translate their dreams into reality. Not only joy to the landowner either, but a cause of rejoicing throughout the Highlands as the new rich were to splurge enormous sums of money on building grandiose lodges and, in some cases, great castles, in the Scottish baronial style; this gave employment first to the builders and then to the vast staff which had to be employed to keep the house and gardens up to the style which the owners not only required but could amply afford, due to the profits being generated from Lowland or English factories.

One of the perverse things about the Scots is their inability to recognise the vital role played in the economics of the Highlands by such absentee owners – then and, indeed, now. The absentee landlord is a figure constantly attacked in the press of modern Scotland, and yet, from an economic point of view, it is a jolly good thing he is absentee; it means he must employ a factor to oversee his affairs while he is away; a housekeeper (or couple) to look after the house; a gardener to mow the lawn; in fact, people to do all the sort of jobs which if he actually lived on the place full time he might consider doing himself! It also means, of course, that he is earning – of necessity – lots of boodle which he will then cheerfully pour down the throat of his voracious Highland sporting estate.

Without doubt, owning a sporting estate, as we have said, is like standing under a cold shower tearing up five-pound notes; indeed, with inflation, it is more likely to be twenty-pound notes today. Yet rich men still cue up to buy them when they come on the market. Why is a mystery, although I suppose a medium-sized sporting estate, which might eat up between fifty and a hundred thousand pounds a year, may seem cheap when compared with the cost of running a string of racehorses or a large yacht in the South of France; anyway, what is the point of making lots of lolly unless you can waste some of it.

Today, sporting estates are valued less on the area of land they cover than by what they can produce in the way of game, be it grouse, salmon or stags.

A quick glance at the chart below will show that in 1990 the value of Scottish sporting estates soared. The rise, in fishing particularly, had much to do with a wizard new idea called time share, which suddenly became all the rage and made a lot of people a lot of money (the sellers of time shares that is). The

	1980	1990	1992	1997
Salmon fishing (£/fish)	£1,500	£12,000	£7,000	£6,000
Deer stalking (£/stag)	£6,000	£30,000	£15,000	£22,000
Grouse shooting (£/brace)	£450	£3,000	£2,000	£3,000

Source: Strutt & Parker

best time-share schemes (from the sellers' viewpoint) were those which offered a fixed week's fishing on a stretch of river for a fixed period of time (say, thirty years). This was a brilliant scheme from the owner's viewpoint. Previously he had probably let out rods on the river anyway and had borne the entire cost of managing the river out of the rental income. Now he not only got a large up-front capital sum but the time-share owners would take on the management cost of the river, and in thirty years' time the whole thing would fall neatly back into his son's lap.

It has to be said that while initially the punters fell for this hook, line and sinker, it did not take long for the realisation to dawn on them that such schemes were a bit of a rip off; as a result, a lot of over-optimistic and rather greedy owners ceased to find many takers. Time shares, with the week being sold in perpetuity, are still being offered, however, and taken up. Personally, I always feel buying one fixed week's fishing is a very dodgy game, because what looks like a prime week's fishing today might in ten years' time yield nothing. In other words, I think that salmon fishing may be cyclical and that the spring run, which used to be the glory of so many rivers but is now a shadow of its former self, may yet return one year and once again be the jewel in the crown of salmon fishing. If this does happen, those who are now buying relatively inexpensive weeks in May or April may have the last laugh over their richer friends who are punting heavily on weeks in September.

It is Scotland's good fortune that so many rich men still have this love affair with Scotland, but it is good fortune which few if any of the Scots appreciate. Instead they indulge in a long tedious whinge about Scotland being 'bought up by foreigners', conveniently forgetting that in the 1930s a large number of Scotsmen emigrated to England and bought up a large amount of East Anglia for a song, which they then farmed rather efficiently. In other words, what is sauce for the goose is sauce for the gander. The latest whinge is that many of the new owners are not even Englishmen but foreigners from beyond the seas, such as Kjeld Kirk-Christiansen, who runs the Danish Lego company and owns the fifty-thousand-acre Strathconon estate in Ross-shire. Foreigners now own around thirty estates in Scotland. But again my supposition is that these new owners are very rich men and will be happy to plough large amounts of money into their estates, employ many people and be good stewards of their land.

It is salutary to consider the different attitudes of the English to the same problem. In London, for instance, some sixty to seventy per cent of houses and flats in the smarter areas of London are now owned or occupied by foreigners, yet I cannot recall ever reading in the English press any demands that foreigners should be deterred from buying property in England.

It would be nice to think that the Scottish Parliament will leave the subject of land well alone but I am afraid that this is unlikely. The first signs of the storm about to break over the Highlands are already there. The Scottish Office have set up a 'Land Reform Group', and among the areas it is looking into are:

The availability of information on landownership
The balance of the rights of landowners and public interest
Standards of land management; enforcing or encouraging
    standards
Assistance of community ownership
Disposal and acquisition of land by public bodies

While the members of this group sit around scratching their heads the Scottish Office has also issued a discussion paper called 'Towards a Development Strategy for Rural Scotland'. So, as you can see, in 1998 it is all go in Scotland. It will be interesting to see what comes of it all. The only certainties are that, whatever 'strategy' is produced, the long-term effect on the rural economy of Scotland will be virtually zero and buckets of public money will have been wasted. This in itself is nothing new, but what could be far more dangerous is if they start persecuting the absentee landowner, who remains – as he has been for nearly a hundred years – the principal goose that lays the golden eggs in the Highlands and Islands.

Meanwhile plans are afoot for Scotland to have its own National Parks. This is sad as Scotland has so much beautiful untamed wild country it seems a pity to wreck any of it by calling it a National Park. The chairman of Scottish National Heritage is jubilant and says: 'The creation of National Parks for Scotland is an exciting opportunity to ensure the future of some of our best loved places.' My reply to this is if any reader has a 'best loved place' in one of the three areas currently proposed – the Cairngorns, the Trossachs and Loch Lomond – he'd better get there fast before it is ruined, and his peaceful contemplation of its beauty is forever interrupted by hoards of people getting off coaches, demanding toilet blocks and refreshment kiosks, and the mountainside is dotted with ramblers in their brightly coloured kagools.

Once an area becomes a National Park it is cursed with a budget which must be spent. As the people who run National Parks are only human, what they want in the future is bigger budgets, and the way to achieve this is to popularise the park; as more and more people visit, so you can justifiably claim you need more and more money to build 'facilities' for them, while at the same time getting plaudits from everyone. Then comes the magic moment when you produce a report claiming that there are now too many people using the park and you can demand yet more money to restore worn footpaths, build 'honeypot attractions' and so on. In short, the one thing National Parks don't do is what they are meant to do, 'safeguard areas of wilderness'.

True, Scotland is not thinking of copying the English template when it comes to National Parks; instead they are looking at one 'which is tailored to the Scottish situation'. Well, I live in hopes that they will get it right, but frankly I doubt it.

One of the myths ably propagated by elements of the Scottish press is that owners of Highland estates are selfish and have no desire to develop them economically; they are happy to sit on thousands of acres of barren land purely for their own personal enjoyment. It is true that there may be a small minority who take this attitude, but to be able to do so they need to be very rich men who employ large numbers of people to satisfy their every whim. The majority of owners undoubtedly rack their brains constantly for ideas which will result in their being able to boast that their estate makes money. Sometimes, as in England, misconceived investment decisions are taken which end up being the cause of the eventual sale and break-up of the estate – the late Simon Fraser's attempt to start a water-bottling plant being a recent classic example.

It is not surprising, given such examples of unfortunate and loss-making investment projects in the Highlands, that many owners have fallen back on what they know and understand and have concentrated their resources on offering sporting holidays to fishermen, stalkers and shooting parties. The attractions of such holidays in Scotland are obvious, and the money they bring in substantial. The Carnarvon Report of 1992 estimated that sporting estates provided about 2,200 full-time job equivalents and that the direct expenditure on countryside sports in Scotland, valued at 1990 prices, was as follows:

Salmon fishing	£39m *(by participants)*
Sporting shooting	£115 m *(by providers and participants)*
Grouse shooting	£10m *(by providers)*
Stalking – Highland deer forests	£9.0 m *(by providers)*

The continuing efforts of many owners to make their estates pay, or at least break even, through providing traditional sporting holidays to rich tourists are not only economically beneficial but also environmentally so. The income brought in enables owners to manage the heather-clad hills of Scotland in a way which encourages grouse but is also of value to a great many other forms of wildlife, while the rivers of Scotland benefit from having vigilant owners who work hard to ensure that one of their prime assets is kept in good health. It is, as ever, one of the great ironies that owners of such places instead of being praised for preserving the landscape are likely to be penalised by having layers of bureaucracy heaped upon them and planning restrictions put on their every improvement.

Those who blame private landowners for the relative economic failure of much of the Highlands and Islands are long on criticism but short on effective solutions. Many of the solutions proposed by planners have not proved a success and it is chilling to consider what much of the Highlands would be like today if all estates had been nationalised after the war and left to the tender mercies of central planners. Many, one suspects, of Scotland's wilderness areas would have been planted wholesale by the Forestry Commission, implementing what, back in the 1950s, was 'the preferred solution' to the upland areas of Great Britain. For those of you who are puzzled today as to why this was, the reason was simple – it was assumed that forestry would provide large-scale employment. The Forestry Commission's main worry at the time was how they were going to recruit and house the estimated fifty thousand men they were going to need to employ in the Kielder Forest by the year 2000. Now, as that year approaches, they employ directly no more than five hundred men in that forest! They had, in short, failed to foresee the technological advances which would make ninety-nine out of every hundred proposed jobs redundant over the next forty years.

Sadly, the last fifty years have been littered with failed schemes – aluminium smelting works powered by cheap hydro-electricity, pulp mills and so on. Meanwhile, as 'quick fix', grant-funded industries have failed one after another, many estates have managed to plod on, doing what they know best and do best and keeping alive, all to Scotland's considerable economic benefit.

CHAPTER 8

The Common Agricultural Policy

The very words Common Agricultural Policy (CAP) are enough to make the most insomniac among us go to sleep. But no book on the British countryside can avoid mentioning a policy which has had such an far-reaching effect on the structure of the British countryside and on the incomes of farmers and landowners. Love it or hate it, the CAP is an integral part of rural Britain and, this being the case, a basic knowledge of it, and its background, is essential.

The reason for the existence of the CAP is simple and in America they have a very good phrase to describe it – pork-barrel politics. Back in 1962, when the CAP was effectively born, West Germany and France had, respectively, twenty and forty per cent of their population in farming. However, that twenty per cent in Germany was an extremely important segment of the electorate. About ninety per cent of them were Catholics and routinely voted Christian Democrat and, at the time the CAP was being put together, who do you think was in power in Germany? – why the Christian Democrats of course.

Germany also had a history of agricultural protectionism stretching right back to the days of Bismark, who had introduced tariffs to protect German farmers in the nineteenth century. The result was that German farms were small and chronically inefficient – as indeed most of them still are. In the 1950s only one fifth of one per cent of German farms were larger than a hundred hectares!

It was, in fact, not till 1967 that the CAP was actually up and running. Negotiations between the various EEC countries had been long and tortuous as each fought for its own interests. The eventual result was, predictably, an economic shambles.

The method of subsidy decided on by the EEC was guaranteed

prices. In simplistic terms, the CAP guaranteed the price of all farmers' production but the cost would not, as in Britain under the deficiency-payment system, be borne by the taxpayer – instead it would be passed on to the consumer in higher prices. This was, on the face of it, a clever move as it made the cost of subsidising farmers virtually invisible. That was the plan; unfortunately what the brains behind it forgot was that if you guaranteed prices then production would inexorably rise. As an illustration, between 1965 and 1991 consumption of food in the UK increased by 0.1% per annum while production rose by nearly 2% per annum.

The UK has not been unique in this respect. Throughout the EEC demand was, and is, rising significantly slower than production. The predictable result has been the arrival on the scene of beef mountains and wine lakes and so on. Initially these 'surplus' foods were sold into intervention and stored, at great cost to the EU, who hoped that a series of bad harvests or some other act of God would allow them to unload them back on the market sometime in the future. When God proved uncooperative, the great brains of the then EEC decided to sell them on the world market and invented export subsidies.

In effect the EEC paid exporters the difference between the intervention price in Europe and the world-market price in order to enable exporters to flog the stuff outside the Common Market. Needless to say, this did not exactly endear the EEC to other exporting nations, who saw the world price fall because of the quantities of EEC-subsidised grain flooding the open market.

All of these actions caused the cost of running the EEC to escalate out of control so that currently it is approximately thirty billion pounds per annum. The budgetary cost is only one aspect of the economic cost to the EEC as a whole, another is the extra cost of buying food shoved on to the shoulders of every citizen of the European Union. The following table shows a comparison of prices in 1991.

In 1991 the National Consumer Council estimated that the CAP cost £110 a year per head of population in higher prices, as well as a further £59 per year in higher taxes, giving an annual cost to a family of four of around £680 per year. A not inconsiderable

	UK wholesale	World market
Butter – pence per 250g	47p	19p
Beef (topside) – pence per kg	178p	112p
Sugar – pence per kg	37p	12p

Source: National Consumer Council (NCC)

amount, you will agree, and yet there is a total lack of protest by consumers at this enormous tax charge which they meekly bear. The reason, of course, is that the tax is invisible.

Admittedly these costs to both consumers and taxpayers are arguable. For instance, as we have already said, without the surplus EU production pumped on to the world market, world-market prices for many commodities would be higher and the saving to the consumer less. However, that there is a substantial cost is not an issue, everyone agrees on that at least, the question is how big it is, and virtually no one agrees on that. Estimates vary from a high of £1,500 per annum for a family of four right down to a few hundred pounds.

But the cost of the CAP is not just borne by the consumer or taxpayer it is also borne by new entrants into the farming industry. Long-term subsidies, such as those available to farmers under the CAP, have a major economic drawback – they become capitalised in the price of land. Let me explain. The price of agricultural land is intrinsically linked to the potential income which it generates. It is true that over the last twenty-five years various seemingly intelligent people have invested in land because, as Mark Twain said, 'God isn't making it anymore.' They assumed for this reason that the price of land would rise regardless of its profitability. Most of these people bought on behalf of City institutions and the like – as did Jim Slater, the City financier who, in 1973, told his agent to go out and buy land, and when asked by his agent when he should stop, said: 'When you reach the sea.' It would be an interesting exercise to work out just how much money City institutions have lost in investing in land over the last thirty years.

The fact is, the price of land continually demonstrates that only one thing really matters and that is its potential for producing income. So high subsidies get transposed into higher rents and into higher land prices. In other words, it could be argued, that someone who buys a farm at today's inflated land prices receives no benefit at all from farm subsidies, as the price he pays for his land reflects the value of the current level of subsidies. For example, in a 'non-subsidised' farming environment the price of land instead of being, say, £3,000 per acre would be only £600–£1,000 per acre, so a 'new entrant' is, in fact, paying around £2,000 per acre for the subsidies.

Clearly, as people, relying on the continuation of high subsidies, make investment decisions, such as buying land or investing in new buildings and machinery, then the pressure for those subsidies to remain grows; without them many farmers' businesses would become uneconomic and the banks, who lent them the money to fund their expansion, would find, as they did way back in the 1930s, that lending on farmland was a high-risk occupation.

However, the gross excesses of the CAP have had another major detrimental effect on farmers and landowners. Back in the 1940s and right up to the early 1970s farmers were hailed as the heroes of British industry. Newspapers ran leading articles praising farmers for achieving higher and higher productivity and contrasting the abject performance of British industry with the brilliant efforts of British agriculture.

All that has changed. I cannot recall the last time I read anything positive about British farming in the newspapers. Instead farmers are held up as being heavily feather-bedded scroungers – always with their hand out asking for more money and, when they get the money, using it to destroy yet more of the unique environment of the British countryside. I am not saying I agree with that image, but that is how farmers are now perceived by the vast majority of the public. If British farmers get bad PR it is nothing to what the whole CAP manages to attract. The system is riddled with fraud; independent estimates calculate that fraud accounts for around ten per cent of the total CAP budget. Inevitably, most of this fraud occurs in the southern European countries such as Spain, Italy, Portugal and Greece. The seeming inability of the EU to take steps to stamp out malpractices in these countries is yet more evidence that the EU is still a pork-barrel organisation where bribery and corruption is rife. The truth of the matter is, as a businessman friend of mine, Sir Benjamin Slade, so aptly puts it, you should never do business with any country where they don't wear overcoats or where they have green in their flag. What is it, I wonder, that makes the southern Europeans inherently corrupt?

For any industry to get such a consistently bad press is disastrous, especially when only two per cent of the population is engaged in agriculture. It can be argued that as the CAP is a European policy there is little the UK government can do about it anyway, so the disastrous public image of UK agriculture is not strictly relevant. But this view fails to take account of the vast changes which have occurred in Europe and the enormous reduction there has been in the numbers employed in French and German agriculture. The percentage of their populations involved in agriculture has now fallen to around three per cent in Germany, five per cent in France, seven per cent in Italy and a little over ten per cent in Spain. As the numbers in farming fall, so the influence farmers have on politicians wanes in direct proportion.

The bad PR of farmers and landowners has not been helped by the leaders of such bodies as the NFU who consistently defend the indefensible. Remarks such as 'someone has to be paid to look after the countryside' are, frankly, rubbish. The harsh truth is that in a subsidy-free world the price of land might well fall dramatically and put many farmers out of business, but the fall in land values would encourage new entrants who, because of the cheapness of land, would be able to farm profitably. Such a scenario would probably lead to an acceleration of the current trend towards larger farms as farmers took advantage of cheap land to achieve greater economies of scale.

Part of the reason for the fall from public favour of farmers has been the growing interest in what are loosely called 'environmental issues'. Farmers are viewed by the general public as being overtly aggressive in improving their farms and boosting their profitability and as a result are deemed to be contributing to what is sometimes called the 'desertification' of the countryside. It is true that the arable acreage has expanded enormously over the last thirty years in response to higher prices for arable crops at a time when higher yielding varieties of wheat make four tons an acre a realistic target for a large number of farmers.

But much of the real damage environmentally has been caused by one of the principle aims of the original CAP which was 'to ensure a fair standard of living for the agricultural population'. This has been translated over the years into making large grants available to farmers in the poorer parts of the country and in areas of poor land enabling them to 'improve' such land. Inevitably this meant that wetlands were drained, upland grassland 'improved' and so on. The advent of livestock subsidies, in the form of 'headage' payments to those in the uplands (designated as Less Favoured Areas or LFAs), also resulted in a major expansion of the sheep flock in the UK which led – predictably – to over grazing and much environmental damage. Eventually, the powers that be woke up to what was happening and recognised that the end result was perhaps not so marvellous after all, and so invented various schemes like ESAs (Environmentally Sensitive Areas), SSSIs (Sites of Special Scientific Interest) and Country Stewardship Schemes which all aimed to pay farmers money not to farm in an 'environmentally' unfriendly way – a way, incidentally, in which they would never have contemplated farming in the first place but for the large number of grants and subsidies which encouraged them to do just that – a truly *Alice in Wonderland* situation and one which only a body like the EU could create.

The mountains of surplus food meant that even the EU came to realise by the early 1980s that it could not continue on its chosen course. Faced with effectively two ways to reduce food surpluses – drop prices or control production – it chose the latter and invented quotas for dairy farmers and set-aside for cereal growers.

Inevitably these reforms were energetically opposed by the farming lobby but the end result has in fact been extremely beneficial to farmers. Quotas it was soon discovered had a value and could be traded. This had not, of course, been an intention when they were introduced but farmers and land agents soon found a way round the rules and regulations and a thriving market in leasing and selling quotas was soon established and farmers found to their amazement and gratification that they were the owners of substantial capital sums in the form of the value of their quotas. This ability to conjure enormous quantities of money out of thin air and make a present of it to farmers is something the EU is particularly good at.

In fairness to the EU, dairy quotas have achieved the aim of removing the butter mountain and set-aside did play a role in restricting cereal production and thus contributing to the high price of grain in 1994–6. However it is surely an absurdity of the quota system that the United Kingdom with some of the best grass-growing land in Europe is only allowed to produce eighty per cent of its dairy requirement.

Set-aside and quotas were just tinkerings with the engine of the CAP; come the early 1990s, it was realised that a full-scale reform of the whole system was needed, not least because the USA, as a major agricultural exporter, was fast losing patience with the way the EU's subsidised exports were driving down world prices and stealing the market share of its own farmers.

In 1991 the inevitable wholesale reform was finally mooted by the Agricultural Commissioner, Raymond MacSharry. Just as inevitably the final reforms, which were agreed in May 1992, were very much watered down. In effect, the reforms managed to avoid touching controversial areas – such as the enormous subsidies given to Italians to grow sub-standard tobacco – and concentrated their fire on the grain sector.

The end result was a mixed package of measures: support prices for grain were to be cut by 29% over three years with farmers offered acreage payments (Arable Area Aid), providing they placed at least 15% of their grain-growing area in set-aside. In simplistic terms this represented a major change of direction for the CAP – a departure from subsidies aimed at encouraging production and a swing to subsidies on acreage regardless of the level of production.

In fact, the MacSharry reforms were to herald a major boom in farming incomes, and once again proved, if proof were needed, that long-term plans made by bureaucrats are almost always fatally flawed. MacSharry and his team had not considered the unthinkable – that world grain prices would rise. So farmers in the golden years of 1994, 1995 and 1996 watched in amazement as the world price for wheat soared to in excess of £120 per ton by mid-1996 as opposed to the forecast price for wheat in 1996 of £88 per ton. At the same time, the devaluation of the pound caused by Black Monday resulted in the compensatory payments to farmers in the UK, which had been set in ecus, rising considerably, so instead of receiving a forecast £86 per acre Arable Area Aid they got about £110 an acre.

Hardly surprising then that farmers rejoiced and, as ever with farmers when the good times arrive, rushed out and started spending money on more land and machinery – saving for a rainy day not being an attribute which most farmers possess. So farmland prices soared away into the stratosphere, as did rents on New Farm Business Tenancies.

Come 1997 and the gathering storm broke. Prices of wheat went into free fall ending up at around £75 per ton, the pound strengthened dramatically against European currencies and suddenly the smile was wiped off the face of the agricultural community.

The knowledge that the year 2000 will bring yet new reforms of the CAP only adds to the misery. The debate and proposals are as yet in their infancy and the history of the CAP tells us that what is initially put forward normally bears little resemblance to the actual outcome. None the less, the next set of CAP reforms are likely to be radical if for no better reason than that they have to be if the European Union is to achieve its ambitions in extending membership to former Warsaw Pact countries. In short, the EU would bankrupt itself if it made available similar subsidies to those countries' farmers as it at present gives to its own farmers.

Perhaps one of the most worrying aspects of the proposals is the suggestion that area compensatory payments, such as Arable Area Aid, should be limited to small farmers – an idea, which, in

Euro-speak, is called modulation; basically, the concept, which appears to have the backing of the present Labour government, is that farmers should be limited in the total amount of subsidy they receive. This is clearly a device aimed at British farmers as the vast majority of large farmers in the EU are based in the UK. MacSharry tried this trick in 1992, but the then Minister of Agriculture protested vehemently. It is debatable whether a Labour minister will oppose such a measure; I am inclined to think that payments such as Arable Area Aid will be restricted to smaller farms and the size of subsidy cheque to individual farmers capped. The question is at what level this cap will be? My guess is around £50,000. The next question is how will it be administered? If a man with a 2000-acre farm gives 500 acres to his wife, 500 acres to his son and keeps a 1,000 acres for himself will that land – still farmed as a whole, but producing three separate sets of accounts – be counted as one farm of 2,000 acres or three separate units? An interesting question and we must wait and see what the answer is.

Meanwhile the end result of the reforms, married with the phasing out of set-aside both in Europe and the United States, must mean weak grain prices for some years to come. History suggests that if weak grain prices are translated into a cutback in the area planted, the price will firm up eventually, but that is something which must still be some years away.

Looking into my crystal ball, I regard the future of subsidised agriculture in Europe to be grim. A falling percentage of the population involved in farming across the developed economies in Europe means – bluntly – that farming's political clout is decreasing and it is hardly likely that farmers will continue to receive such largesse forever.

There is a faint ray of hope, however. Perhaps today's world food surplus will become tomorrow's world food shortage. Consider the awakening economies of South-East Asia and China. Over a fifteen-year period, during which the economy boomed, South Korea changed from a relatively backward country into a fully developed Western-style society, the consumption of meat per head of population trebled and the consumption of grain per head of population doubled. Now

South Korea is a small country but China is a vast one, home to around a quarter of the world's population. Currently it aims to feed itself and is between 90–95% self-sufficient in grain, producing around 490 million tons (1996). Assume, for the sake of argument, that China achieves, in economic terms, over the next twenty years what Korea did over fifteen, and then assume that its consumption of food products rises as Korea's did, and you have an interesting scenario: China could, within the next twenty-five years, be importing some 300 million tons of grain per annum.

China itself predicts that its grain consumption will rise, by the year 2030, by 150 million tons per annum, but this is because of an anticipated population growth from 1.2 billion to 1.6 million by that date. In other words, the Chinese are not taking into account any increase in consumption due to changed economic affluence of the population leading to altered eating habits, as has happened in every other Asian economy which has been successful.

While it is true that the world is at present (1998) producing a world surplus of cereals, it is worth noting that in four out of seven years – between 1990 and 1997 – the world produced less grain than there was demand for, hence the farming boom years. With current world production at around 1.48 billion tons of grain and consumption at 1.40 billion tons the gap is a relatively minuscule one of less than 5% or around 80–100 million tons.

It is, of course, true that over the last thirty-five years average grain yields per acre have nearly doubled, but it must be extremely doubtful if that trick can be performed again. There is also the much hyped potential for increasing yields in the vast wheat lands of Russia and the Ukraine and other ex-Soviet-block countries. The potential is indeed there but by the time it is realised it is likely that the economies of these countries will themselves have recovered sufficiently for their own grain consumption per head to have increased in line with extra yield from the at present under-exploited farmland. In other words, planned-for surpluses might not be available after all.

But the extra demand caused by the economic improvement of 25% of the world population – conceivably 40% if India ever gets its act together – is not the only factor. The world population is also set to grow at some 900 million people per decade for the next forty years. And as, at present, every human being consumes on average 0.25 tons of grain per head, world production will have to rise by some 225 million tons per decade to feed so many mouths.

The above scenario has, of course, been mapped out before. In the late eighteenth century the economist Thomas Malthus, for one, predicted doom and gloom on the basis of a rising population and the limited capacity of man to feed himself. He has been proved wrong for the last two hundred years, but that is not to say he won't one day be proved right.

A further question mark hangs over the continued productivity of much of the land brought into production round the world by irrigation. A build-up of salt is threatening the fertility of much of this land and it may be that yields in many irrigated areas will fall over the next twenty-odd years.

I have not touched on the much debated 'greenhouse effect' and the global warming necessarily attendant upon it. This is mainly because I am sceptical about the scientific analysis. But clearly if it did happen the effect on world agriculture would be dramatic in the extreme.

So far we have taken what might be called the bullish view on the long-term future of farming, but what of the other side of the coin? Well, bears will point out that we have hitherto managed to feed the world; *ergo* we will continue to do so; scientific advances in types of crops, aided by the genetic revolution, will allow new high-yielding varieties to be developed quickly and to flourish, perhaps in environments previously hostile to grain production, and maybe science will pull off another miracle like the green revolution of the 1960s, when new high-yielding types of rice banished hunger from much of Asia.

It is a race and it remains to be seen who the winners will be. For the last two hundred years the scientists and agricultural improvers have consistently managed to keep agricultural production ahead of the demand of rising populations – the question is, will they manage to achieve the same trick over the next thirty-odd years? It is perhaps worth bearing in mind that the reason Malthus's predictions have remained unfulfilled has more to do with his lack of knowledge of geography than with any ignorance of economics. He had no idea of the vast virgin lands in North America and Australia waiting to be discovered and could never have imagined the improvements in transport and machinery which would allow these large tracts of land to be economically exploited.

So we are left wondering how different the picture of farming in this country in twenty years will be. It could be that the CAP will have long since ceased to exist as a way of subsidising farmers and will have metamorphosed into an organisation which forces farmers to sell their valuable crops at an artificially low price to European consumers and only allows surplus production to be sold at the far higher world-market price!

Come to think about it, I am sure that is what will happen. For centuries, governments have intervened in agriculture and food. For the last fifty-odd years that intervention has ostensibly been in the interests of the farmer against the consumer. Perhaps in thirty years' time it will be the consumers' turn to benefit?

One thing is sure, the future of British agriculture will depend less and less on decisions made by the domestic government, or even the EU in Brussels, and more and more on events outside their control in faraway places such as China and the old Soviet Union, as well as on what scientists dream up in their laboratories.

CHAPTER 9

The Woodlands and Forestry

Trees are an excrescence upon earth provided
by God for the payment of debts.

SAMUEL PEPYS (1633–1703)

I suppose that we live in a time when 'short-term' investments
are everyone's ideal. People are keen to make a quick buck and
then either retire or move on to the next enterprise. Well,
forestry is the ultimate long-term investment. I am now cutting
down oak trees my ancestor planted to provide the timber to
build ships in which someday to beat the French. Sadly ships
are today made of steel and the French are now a protected
species.

Such is the long-term nature of the investment. It is also a
good example of how quite often the markets for which the
timber was intended have entirely disappeared by the time the
trees are ready to cut. When that happens many owners often
give up and woods become neglected. Many estates have
hundreds of acres of neglected broadleaved woods and are at a
loss to know what to do with them. It is one of the major failures
of British forestry policy since the war that no serious effort has
been made to tackle this problem. Actually that is not quite fair
as until recently the solution was to fell them and replant with
conifers. Now the chances of getting permission to do that is on
a par with getting an iced drink in the middle of the desert. But
while on the one hand government forbids you to carry out the
only economic solution to neglected woods, on the other it
offers no alternative solution.

This is a pity as there is value in most timber, the trick is
getting it out. The concentration over much of the last fifty
years on softwood production has meant that the marketing and

selling of the UK's hardwoods has received little attention. In short, what is required is a national body to carry out research and development in timber products and then to sell those products to the architects and builders who are the end users. Instead we have money being thrown around in penny packets at various worthy local initiatives run, on the whole, by enthusiastic environmentalists who know little about the business of timber or the art of marketing.

But let's leave the contentious subject of neglected broad-leaved woodland for a moment and look at the history of forestry over the last half century or so.

The average estate will have a mixed bag of woodland depending on previous owners' views on forestry. Estate owners after the Second War broadly fell into two categories – those who believed forestry could be the way to the promised land of making estates pay and building up a large capital sum, and those who despaired about the whole thing and either did nothing or leased their woods to the Forestry Commission on nine-hundred-and-ninety-nine-year leases.

Most estate woods were ravaged during the First War when the demand for timber soared (all those duck boards needed in the trenches, not to mention pit props for mines, huts for troops, wooden chassis for vehicles, aircraft frames, etc.) and the government found to its dismay that UK timber resources were negligible. Landowners everywhere were forced to sell their trees to the nation and after the war only a few had the resources or the energy to replant their decimated woodland. What good broadleaved woodland which was left after 1918 was, in all likelihood, felled during the Second World War. The end result of all this devastation was not only that the forests were wrecked but that the industry which existed to process and market the hardwoods grown was also doomed as, come 1945, there was little good raw material left for it to handle.

The lack of a major hardwood industry in the UK today is a direct result of the toll extracted from Britain's forests during two world wars, and the lesson for politicians and environ-mentalists is that a forest industry is like a huge oil tanker – it needs ten miles of sea-room to stop. The economic consequences of decisions made today about forestry may not become apparent till a hundred years have passed.

The forests we see today owe much to the policies enacted by the Labour government of 1945–50. At the end of the Second War a new generation of owners returned from the fighting and some, fired up by the Forestry Act of 1947, which offered grants for planting and maintenance of plantations, became enthusiastic foresters. Trees became the 'in thing' in landowning circles and aged woodland workers, who for years had done little except sweep the drives, trim the laurel and provide firewood for the house, found themselves put to work planting, weeding, beating up and brashing new plantations. It must have been for some a severe shock to the system, for others a new lease of life.

Apart from the advent of grants a further incentive was that woods managed with the long-term aim of being a commercial enterprise could be assessed under Schedule D for income tax purposes – in effect, that meant that all expenditure on such woods could be set against other income for tax purposes. At a time of high marginal tax rates the attractions were obvious. Technically, of course, although woods could benefit from Schedule D in the growing stage, once they were felled and produced income, profits would be taxed. However, as on change of ownership the new owner could opt to switch from Schedule D to Schedule B, which meant that expenditure could not be set against other income for tax purposes but that profits were tax free, this was not a problem. Trees, even coniferous ones, take at least twenty-five years from the time of planting to the time when they begin to produce profits in the form of thinnings, so if the original owner had not died in the period, he could transfer the ownership of the plantations, as they came into profit, into his son's name, and his son could elect for a change of schedule.

There was one other significant advantage taxwise to woodlands – they did not attract death duties. It would have been ludicrous if they had. How could death duties, or Inheritance Tax as it is now called, be levied on a crop which, in the form of coniferous timber, takes roughly fifty years to mature, and for species such as oak, over one hundred and twenty years? If death duties had been levied the end result would have been the wholesale destruction of the very woods the government was so anxious for landowners to plant, as their heirs would have been forced to fell semi-mature woods to pay the tax.

This last benefit of woods was not lost on some of the more astute landowners. Several estates saved themselves a fortune in death duties when doctors told some aged peer that he had only six months to live and he went on the spending spree to end all spending sprees buying up forests the length and breadth of the country. The system was relatively easy and especially beneficial if he borrowed the money to do it. Say he borrowed a £100,000 to buy woods; that £100,000 would count as a debit item on his heirs eventual death-duty bill while the assets which it had bought – the forests – would have been tax free and could be sold to pay the tax bill on the rest of the estate.

Thus a renaissance in estate forestry occurred, fuelled by a mixture of grants and tax relief. It is worth reflecting that today, in 1998, fifty years after that Act of Parliament, the trees which it inspired are only now being cut. Of course, most owners have throughout history planted trees to provide future profits for their descendants, forestry being the ultimate in long-term investment planning. Samuel Pepys' description of trees as provided by God 'for the payment of debts' was not so wide of the mark. Trees are indeed a very useful way of storing cash for that rainy day.

There are those, however, for whom it is a matter of jam tomorrow, jam yesterday, but never jam today. Many wood owners have given up waiting for the promised profits from their fathers' forestry efforts to enrich them and have become disillusioned by the whole business, repeating *ad nauseam* when you ask them about their woods, which their father lavished so much time and attention on: 'Oh, there is no money in forestry.'

This negative attitude is in part due to the removal of Schedule D tax relief on forestry in the 1986 budget. This came as a blow to those with traditional estate woodlands. Following their practice in farming the home farm, many landowners had found it conveniently easy, for tax purposes, to put part of the gamekeepers' and gardeners' salaries down against expenditure on woods. The sudden realisation that every one pound they spent on their trees was now one pound out of taxed income gave them a rude shock from which most, ten years later, have still not recovered.

Of course, the reason they don't make profits today is relatively easy to spot. Landowners and their advisers have, like the dodo, failed to move with the times. In the bad old days before Mrs Thatcher, top rates of income tax regularly exceeded 90% and in 1979 were at 98%. Expenditure on woodlands, therefore, was not a big issue for a high-rate taxpayer as the taxman effectively picked up more than 90% of the bill. Landowners became lazy and forest-management companies became rich as there was little incentive for woodland owners to scrutinise their expenses in relation to the woodland account. Now, with no tax relief on expenses but tax-free profits to be had on woodland income, there is every reason for a landowner to take a greater interest in the management of his woodlands – but few do, preferring instead to cry into their soup and ceaselessly moan, 'There's no money in trees.' Which is true if you insist on paying large sums to outside managers to do the work for you.

After all, qualified foresters have to be paid and paid well, so who pays them? Why the landowner, who is then disgusted with the small amount of money he receives for the timber his father planted fifty years ago.

The solution is obvious – learn to do most of the management tasks in your own woods yourself. That this simple remedy has failed to register in the minds of so many owners is, I am afraid, not very flattering to the overall intelligence of the average owner.

To illustrate the point let us look at a coniferous plantation of fifteen years standing, coming up to what is called 'first thinning stage'. Now the purpose of thinning woods is quite simple. Initially more trees are planted than required for a final crop; close proximity encourages them to grow fast, to suppress the undergrowth beneath them and to self-prune themselves. However, unless we are going to end up with a rubbishy crop of

softwood in fifty years' time (like most of the Forestry
Commission plantations, of which more later), we need to thin
them out at regular intervals to give them space to put on girth
as well as height.

This is an expensive process. The product from first and
second thinnings goes normally for pulp or chipboard, and the
price paid is unlikely to be much better than £26 a ton delivered
in. Now if you employ a professional forestry management
company to do the work for you they will charge at least £30 per
hour to mark up your timber and in some cases up to £80 an
hour, a commission of five per cent normally on the total value
of the sale, plus supervisory fees, etc.

Now as the costs to the landowner of the professional comes
out of net income it follows that if he is paying someone £80 an
hour it is the equivalent of at least £120 gross and I very much
doubt if many landowners have ever been paid £120 per hour in
their lives to do anything. In other words, if they got off their
arses and went on a few days' training they might find to their
amazement that there actually was jam today in their woods.
Their attitude is the harder to understand as many of them are
not only woodland owners but also working farmers. As such
they should realise that their view of forestry as an investment
is akin to a farmer looking at a field of winter wheat in March
and moaning: 'There is no money in wheat.' Nor there is till the
crop is ripe and safely harvested and in the barn. In other words,
trees will only produce substantial profits when they are mature
and ready for cutting. But the farming analogy does not just
stop here. A farmer knows that once he has sown his field of
wheat the work has only just begun. There is much to be done to
the land between planting and harvesting it if he is going to
maximise his profit and produce a high-yielding quality crop.
Yet the same man will often assume that a tree – once planted –
can be left alone to look after itself, and will not spend any
money or time on giving it any aftercare. The end result is that
his descendants will be left with a worthless messy wood fit only
for firewood.

Of course the removal of the Schedule D tax relief in the 1986
budget was forced by a ground swell of public opinion, carefully

orchestrated in the press, against the planting of alien species of coniferous trees, especially in parts of the far north of Scotland. In fairness much of the press criticism was justified; a lot of the planting taking place was not good forestry and was being carried out solely as a tax-avoidance scheme.

The reasons for the fall from grace, in the public's eyes, of the government-sponsored dash for growth in forestry is, as ever, simple. The government gives tax breaks and grants aimed at private landowners to help them solve a problem. Somewhere in some office in the City of London a canny accountant mulls over the news and, as sure as eggs is eggs, he will twist and turn a eminently praiseworthy government initiative into a perverse tax-avoidance scheme for some of his least deserving clients, thus bringing the whole thing into disrepute and damaging an industry. But what does he care? He's picked up a fat fee.

Actually it is doubtful whether most of his clients will ever get much benefit from their forestry investment. As usual the men who will certainly have made money will be the accountant who advised his client in the first place, the agent who sold the land and the management company which has been looking after it. The humble investor comes, as is so often in 'alternative investment' schemes, a long way down the pecking order. The figures, of course, would have looked good and persuasive on paper but because the client knew nothing about forestry he was often a chicken ripe for plucking.

One forestry experts reckons that twenty-five per cent of the forestry in Scotland is valueless because it will cost more to fell and extract the trees than they are ever going to be worth. This is not surprising if you think about it. Any fool can walk over a hill and plant it up with thousands of seedlings, but when those trees mature you need to get enormous great timber lorries and harvesting machinery into the same plantation.

Commercial forestry – by which I mean actually growing trees with the eventual aim of making a profit out of them – has, as we have said, like commercial farming, received a bad press in recent years. The mainstay of the forestry industry are the so-called exotic species, i.e. coniferous trees. These, with a rotation period of only forty to fifty years, give a good return on

investment, if managed properly. However, the many environmental lobbies have managed to persuade the vast majority of
the population that coniferous trees are a BAD THING. Why this is,
is not quite clear. My own suspicions are that the average punter
is not comparing like with like. In other words, he is shown a
newly planted spruce plantation and then asked whether he
prefers that to a mature oak wood. His answer is obvious.
Strangely if you take a rabid, but uneducated (as most are),
environmentalist into a mature soft-wood plantation, which has
been well managed, the trees thinned and pruned and now, at
fifty years plus, soaring a hundred feet up in the air, and ask him
if he likes what he sees he will wax lyrical with enthusiasm and
be amazed when you tell him that these are the dreaded
coniferous trees.

Today's government, ever ready to bend its policy to the voice
which shouts loudest in its ear, has a forestry policy which, if it
was not so pathetic and disastrously wrong, would be a laugh.
On the one hand, it has announced to the usual fanfare of
publicity, that it wants to double woodland cover in England
over the next fifty years. On the other, it has so structured the
grant system that all that is being planted are 'amenity' woods
and acres of hardwoods which, in all likelihood, will never be of
any economic value whatsoever but will at least guarantee a
gross oversupply of firewood in fifty to a hundred years' time.

This is sad because the UK does have the foundations of a first-
class forestry industry. Currently some thirty-five thousand
people are producing high-quality timber using modern and
extremely efficient timber-processing methods. All this is at
present being put at risk for short-term political gain which, as
timber is a long-term industry, is rather unfortunate and not a
little depressing.

But forestry has become a political hot potato and, at present,
the environmental lobby have the high ground; ignorance is
triumphing over experience. Perhaps the most flagrant example
of ignorance is the introduction of Tree Preservation Orders
(TPOs). They are, as any woodland owner knows, a contradiction
in terms; you can't 'preserve trees'; you can, of course, prolong
their lives till they are completely useless, rotten and then cost a

small fortune to fell, but you cannot prolong their life for ever. The end result of TPOs is that a woodland owner stops carrying out any management of those trees to be preserved as there is no longer anything he can do – they have been effectively 'nationalised'. So what will happen when the big wind next blows and they fall down? Why nothing – the landowner has no money to clear up the damage and replant and no incentive to do either. Of course, many environmentalists would welcome this approach to forest management and enthusiastically point to the amazing natural regeneration which occurred in some woods after the great storm of 1987. That this did happen in some woodland is true, but not all woods react in the same way; soil is critical as far as natural regeneration is concerned. If your wood is on 'greensand', then as soon as a tree falls or is felled and light reaches the forest floor, seedlings will spring up everywhere. If, on the other hand, you are on heavy clay, the only result is likely to be a covering of bramble which will quickly stifle virtually any regeneration.

TPOs are, frankly, selfish short-term solutions. What is needed is Species Preservation Orders which would allow landowners to fell trees providing they replanted with the same species, thus enabling our grandchildren to enjoy the same sight of large mature broadleaved trees as we do today. Commonsense, of course, but commonsense is not something which the environmental lobby has a great store of.

The truth of the matter is that all the woodlands in the UK exist because of one of two reasons. They were either planted for and maintained for field sports or for making money. Often, because the economic reason for the existence of woods has long disappeared they are assumed to be the remnants of some ancient forest and are designated 'ancient woodlands' and surrounded by a plethora of regulations.

A classic instance of this is the steep river-valley banks of Devon, clothed in stunted oak coppice – now virtually valueless as timber but back in the eighteenth century a highly remunerative source of income for landowners. Then they were grown on a twenty-year rotation for bark for the tanning industry. Marshall's *Rural Economy* states:

Formerly, within living memory, four or five pounds an acre
was reckoned a good price for wood of the middle quality
and twenty years' growth. Within the last ten years, or less
time, ten pounds an acre was esteemed a good price for such
wood. Now [1794] it is worth fifteen pounds an acre.

The result of slapping TPOs and other such orders on these
woods is that management by the owners ceases. The canopy
closes in and the woods – instead of being a living, breathing
diverse, natural environment, with some areas clear felled, other
areas in the brushwood stage and some areas mature – becomes
one large monoculture supporting only one form of wildlife.

The current state of regulation and restriction on the forestry
industry by the government via the Forestry Authority is bad
enough, but at least it is carried out by qualified foresters at the
government's expense. Now, a new group has arrived on the
scene determined to impose its own agenda on woodland
owners and yet another layer of costs and bureaucracy.

I refer to those paragons of good conservation and the
environment, the supermarkets and retailers, such as
Sainsbury's, B&Q and W. H. Smith, who, with some forty-odd
other companies, have joined together to form something
called the '95 Group under the aegis of the Forestry
Stewardship Council (FSC) which is part of the Worldwide Fund
for Nature (WWF). The group's stated aim is that by the year
2000 all wood and wood by-products (such as paper) sold in
their stores will come from 'certified' forests. The reasons for
the foundation of the FSC was presumably to help stop the
exploitation and destruction of tropical rain forests, an aim
which few of us would quarrel with. However, the FSC has got
rather carried away and is now seeking to impose those
standards on UK woods – and not just standards. For, if their
aim is implemented, woodland owners will be subject to a
whole raft of bureaucratic forms and professional fees to be
paid to the proverbial 'environmental' stormtroopers who will
carry out the certification process.

Now before I go into this whole question of certification in a
bit more detail – and I promise you all a good laugh, so bear with

me – let us just consider what qualifications companies such as Sainsbury's, B&Q and W. H. Smith have to lecture woodland owners on conservation. Just have a little think for a second. Do they perhaps sell PVC? Or soft-porn books and magazines? Non-returnable bottles? Tin cans? Junk food? Surely not, for these companies must be whiter than white to have taken the stance they have regarding forestry.

So what is their stance? Well the best way to find out is to look at the 'ten principles' of the FSC, reproduced overleaf.

Well, that was all pretty boring, wasn't it? I suppose you are wondering why I felt it was important to quote in full all ten principles? Well, a number of reasons spring to mind.

First, like it or not this is the way the countryside is going – what is being tried on the forest industry today will, in one guise or another, be tried on the farming community tomorrow.

Secondly, it strikes me as a perfect example of the sort of meaningless gibberish, masquerading as English, which those of us in the country have to put up with now from urban-based pressure groups who know f— all about what they are talking about.

Thirdly, of course, those reading it will be wondering what all the fuss is about, as clearly these ten principles do not apply to forestry in the UK – or only if you really stretch a point on one or two of the principles. If you are thinking this you are perfectly right, but completely wrong. Or rather, the FSC thinks you are wrong and wants all owners of productive woodlands in the UK to go through the hoop of applying for certification status.

Fourthly, just cast your mind back to the great and good of British retailing and wonder how they would match up if such standards were required of them by say a Retailers' Stewardship Council (RSC)? Just run through those ten principles and place the word 'retailer' where now stands 'forest management'. Amusing isn't it? Or perhaps you don't find it amusing at all and think that most of the members of the '95 Group must be a complete load of hypocrites.

Fifthly, you may, like me, have got quite excited about principle number 3, the one about indigenous peoples' rights. I expect you thought you might qualify under that heading? Well,

1 **Compliance wth laws and FSC principles**
Forest management shall respect all applicable laws of the country in which they occur, and international treaties and agreements to which the country is a signatory, and comply with all FSC principles and criteria.

2 **Tenure and use rights and responsibilities**
Long-term tenure and use rights to the land and forest resources shall be clearly defined, documented and legally established.

3 **Indigenous peoples' rights**
The legal and customary rights of indigenous peoples to own, use and manage their lands, territories and resources shall be recognised and respected.

4 **Community relations and workers' rights**
Forest-management operations shall maintain or enhance the long-term social and economic wellbeing of forest workers and local communities.

5 **Benefits from the forest**
Forest-management operations shall encourage the efficient use of the forest's multiple products and services to ensure economic viability and a wide range of environmental and social benefits.

6 **Environmental impact**
Forest management shall conserve biological diversity and its associated values, water resources, soils and unique and fragile eco-systems and landscapes, and, by so doing, maintain the ecological functions and integrity of the forest.

7 **Management plan**
A management plan – appropriate to the scale and intensity of the operations – shall be written, implemented and kept up to date. The long-term objectives of management and the means of achieving them shall be clearly stated.

8 **Monitoring and Assessment**
Monitoring shall be conducted – appropriate to the scale and assessment of forest management – to assess the condition of the forest, yields of forest products, chain of custody, management activities and their social and environmental impact.

9 **Maintenance of natural forests**
Primary forests, well-developed secondary forests and sites of major environmental, social or cultural significance shall be conserved. Such areas shall not be replaced by tree plantations or other land use.

10 **Plantations**
(Draft principle for plantations, not yet ratified by FSC membership) Plantations should be planned and managed in accordance with principles 1–9 above, and the following criteria. Such plantations can and should complement natural forests and the surrounding eco-systems, provide community benefits and contribute to the world's demand for forest products

so did I, but sadly apparently not. Being indigenous is apparently a *Catch 22* designation. You can only be considered to belong to this privileged group if you live in an indigenous manner – i.e. as a primitive person. So, presumably, once the native population make enough money out of their forests, because of their indigenous status, to start buying modern goods they then lose this coveted title? However, it does strike me that this is something to keep a watching brief on. With any luck the UK government, or perhaps the EEC, will one day sign some ridiculous document promising to respect 'the legal and customary rights of indigenous people', safe in the knowledge that they do not have any, and then we can take them to court and get the meaning of the word indigenous defined. Who knows, we might win. After all, many landowners' families have lived on the same spot for five hundred years or more and if this does not make them 'indigenous' I don't know what does.

Now, of course, certification is going to be 'voluntary', and there is nothing to stop a woodland owner not joining, but he may have severe difficulties in marketing his timber if he doesn't join. Why? Because remember the '95 Group have made a commitment to buy timber products and by-products only from forests which are certified by the year 2000.

Now take the case of W. H. Smith. If they actually go down this route it means that every item of paper they sell must – by the year 2000 – have either been recycled or come from a certified forest. So the publisher of a soft-porn magazine, for example, which relies on W. H. Smith for a large percentage of its sales, is going to ensure that the paper it uses all comes from such a source. *Ergo* pulp mills will be forced to buy only from certified forests because the buyers of end product insist on it.

You may by now be thinking, 'This certification thing is going to cost a fortune to run and administer' – if so, you are correct. Then you may be wondering, 'Who is going to pay for all this?' One guess is all you are allowed, I am afraid. The retailer, do I hear? – wrong, bottom of the class! No, the entire cost will inevitably fall on the woodland owner.

Already managers at some chipboard and pulp mills are having to spend time and money checking the forest origins of their raw materials at the behest of some of the '95 Group. The end result is that they are having to take that cost and pass it back to the woodland owner.

So how do you get your forest certified? By spending lots of money, thicky, how else? Who do I spend that money with? Why who else but with approved FSC certifiers, and they don't come cheap, either! Expect to pay £450 a day for one of these boys – and, as you will need at least two visits before you get the necessary certificate, and as on one of these visits two of these creatures will have to be present, and as, in addition, you will be subject to a further visit at least every year and, after six years, you will have to go through the whole tedious process again, it will not be cheap.

Of course, none of the above may happen. Woodland owners may be able to continue to manage their woods in the best manner prescribed by the Forestry Authority.

But let's end on a bullish note – and I am bullish about the long-term prospects for commercial forestry. There are several reasons for this. For a start, most of my fellow landowners are depressed about forestry and, as history convincingly demonstrates, my fellow landowners' ability to guess the future right is non-existent. A friend of mine once had a stockbroker who was infallible, his advice was always bloody awful; if he said the market, or a share, was going down it always went up and vice versa. My friend continued to use him because his advice was consistent, even though it was consistently bad. It is so with landowners. Their prognosis of what the future holds is nearly always wrong, so if you do the opposite you have a very good chance of getting the future right.

But there are also good fundamental reasons for thinking that the next fifty years might herald extremely attractive returns in commercial forestry. The price of any product is decided by supply and demand. The demand for timber has remained constant since the 1960s at 0.67 cubic metres of timber and timber by-products per head of the world population per annum. However, the world population is expanding and over the next forty years will increase by about 900 million people per decade. *Ergo* the world demand for timber in forty years' time will be around 2.4 billion cubic metres larger than it is today, or about 65% greater.

And this is not the whole story. People in developed economies consume a greater amount of wood than those in undeveloped countries. In the UK consumption is currently 0.9 cubic metres per head per annum, about 50% greater than the world average. Now, over the next forty years there is a strong likelihood that China, India and other South-East Asian countries will achieve developed status, causing their consumption of timber to rise considerably. In other words, I anticipate that world demand for wood will more than double over the next forty years.

So if demand is going to be strong and rising what about supply? Timber, of course, is what my economist friends call an elastic commodity. In other words, as its price rises so consumers and end users switch to alternative raw materials. For instance, it competes in manufacturing with other substitute raw materials like plastics and steel; as a fuel with oil, coal and gas; and with recycled material for paper and board production. Also, as the price of timber goes up so formerly uneconomic forests suddenly become profitable to fell, thus increasing supply. These factors all act as a break on the cost of timber spiralling out of control.

However, I think it is fair to say that if the economies of Asia do continue to expand at their current rate, then many competing raw materials will enjoy similar price rises to timber. As for recycling, obviously if timber prices rise then this will become more and more attractive and some timber substitutes – such as straw and hemp in paper – may become economic crops; but it must be doubtful whether they can have more than a dampening effect on overall price rises.

The other question mark is over supply. If prices rise it will undoubtedly encourage the exploitation of the vast untapped reserves of timber within the old Soviet Union. This is a potential problem, but it is one of success – i.e. the rise in price has happened. Also serious questions have to be raised about the cost, both on economic and environmental grounds, of the successful harvesting of much of these reserves of timber. A lot will depend on how the Russian economy develops over the next few decades. If – a big if – they can raise themselves out of their current vodka-soaked corruption, then the threat of unplanned exploitation of the Siberian forests decreases.

In summary then, trees are good news and will become even better news financially. Those who plant and nurture commercial forests today will reap substantial benefits in years to come.

CHAPTER 10

Forestry – the State Sector

With some two and a half million acres of land, the Forestry Commission is easily Britain's biggest landowner. It successfully fought off attempts to privatise it in 1989 by calling on an improbable alliance of conservation groups, landowners, ramblers and the like who all, for different reasons, were frightened of the consequences of a privatised forest industry.

This was almost certainly one of the great missed opportunities of its kind and it is likely that the forestry industry will rue the consequences for many a long year. Instead of being privatised the Forestry Commission was split into two divisions – the Forestry Authority, which became responsible for all the regulatory side of the industry, and Forest Enterprise which is supposed to run the Forestry Commission woodlands as a profitable concern.

I say 'supposed' because to date the performance of Forest Enterprise has been pretty dismal and has resulted on the whole in an operating loss – miraculously transformed though his may be by that old accountant's trick of revaluing assets (i.e. existing plantations) and announcing a paper profit. For instance, in their 1992 accounts Forestry Enterprise had an operating loss of £21.1 million but managed to change this into a profit of £60.9 million by using this rather discreditable accounting method! Considering the Forestry Commission has been assiduously planting trees since the 1920s and has consequently many plantations maturing and being felled, this result is frankly pathetic.

The Forestry Commission bestrides the UK forest industry like a great dinosaur, which in many ways it resembles. It has a small brain based in Edinburgh and it takes an inordinate amount of time for a thought, or decision, to make its way from the head to the tail or vice versa. It is a ponderous beast whose great feet squash out flickering sparks of enterprise in the industry as it ranges over the country. It is the relic of a Stalinist past, of the era of 'planning' – now a discredited concept everywhere except within the portals of the Department of the Environment (DOE).

The problem with the Forestry Commission is that it has a dominant position within the UK market, supplying around 40% of the total of UK timber production. This being the case, the reputation of British forest products is highly influenced by what comes out of Forestry Commission plantations; sadly, that reputation is that the UK grows rubbish. This is not surprising, as rubbish is what the Forestry Commission specialises in growing. This has little to do with the type of species planted but a lot to do with how the plantations are managed.

The vast majority of the Forestry Commission plantations are managed on a low-input system. In other words, once a wood is planted, very little further investment will be made in managing that wood until the day it is felled. This form of management, which I call industrial forestry or 'plant-and-forget forestry', results in a low-quality crop of small saw logs after forty or fifty years.

This management regime can be contrasted with that undertaken by many traditional landowners. Their trees are rigorously thinned as they get older to allow their girths to expand, side branches are pruned off and the aim is to produce big high-quality saw logs over a fifty-year period and attract a premium price for the eventual product.

Although timber produced by such management practices does achieve premium prices, these prices are not as high as they might be while most of the UK timber-processing industry is geared to handling the rubbish produced by the largest forest owner – the Forestry Commission.

Sadly the Forestry Commission management system is dominant in British forests and the result is not only that UK timber is widely regarded as low quality, but an even more worrying side effect has been the universally bad press that coniferous plantations receive in the media from environmental pressure groups. They wax critical about 'dead coniferous forests' but there is no reason why coniferous forests should be 'dead' from an environmental angle if they are thinned and managed properly. It is only when they are left, on a 'plant-and-forget' management system, that eventually, as the trees mature, the canopy closes over and all vegetation dies underneath.

In fairness it has to be admitted that in many of the places which the Forestry Commission has planted, 'plant and forget' was probably the best management solution for the site. For if you thin high upland plantations of shallow-rooted conifers you risk letting the wind into the forest and having the whole lot blown down. The criticism is that the Forestry Commission also applied such management techniques to areas of lowland forestry where the risk of wind blow is minimal.

It is perhaps not surprising, or perhaps it is, that an organisation dedicated to producing large amounts of 'industrial' timber should have no interest in marketing. There is no senior executive with either Forestry Enterprise or the Forestry Commission with this responsibility. Perhaps I should make clear that by marketing I don't mean the selling of trees; what I mean is the development of markets for the timber which is produced. In other words, working with other parts of the industry to promote timber products and to research and to develop ways that timber can be used on higher-value products, thus boosting the price you receive for the primary product.

One of the inherent problems with UK forestry is the absence of any large timber-owning company with the financial clout to promote the use of timber and to research ways to substitute timber economically for less environmentally friendly materials. This is a role the Forestry Commission could – and should – have taken on. Its failure to do so is a sad reflection on its management over the last seventy-five years. So the forest industry looks on helplessly as rival products, which are often environmentally unfriendly, such as steel, PVC, plastics, concrete and the like, are assiduously promoted by their manufacturers and win more and more of the market share from traditional wood products. A typical example is the explosion in PVC windows over the last few years at the expense of traditional wooden ones. Who among us has not winced at seeing these excrescences despoiling some period house? Yet the fault lies with the British timber industry which for years palmed off low-quality soft-wood windows, liable to rot, on an unsuspecting public. Hardly surprising that a market was lost; even though the lesson has now been learned and timber windows are as good – if not better – than PVC ones, the advantage can never be recovered.

But it is the Forestry Commission's regulatory role which most concerns private woodland owners. Worrying 'racist' tendencies are surfacing. The new obsession in conservation circles – as far as trees are concerned – is racial purity of seed source. For many it is now not enough that a landowner plants an oak tree; it must be an oak tree grown from an acorn from a 'native tree'. As for planting trees such as beech or sweet chestnut, both of which have been cultivated in this country for at least two thousand years, these are now condemned as 'not native species'. Conservationists sometimes sound remarkably like Adolf Hitler at a Nuremberg Rally. The eventual aim of many conservationists is that all future broadleaf planting will be from a 'native seed source'.

Actually this is scientific and historical nonsense. For centuries landowners have travelled widely and a three-hundred-year-old oak tree is just as likely to be the result of a keen seventeenth-century forester (and there were many of them, as conservationists would know if they ever bothered to read Evelyn's classic, *Sylva*) seeing a fine stand of oak on his travels and filling his pockets with acorns to sow on his estate on his return.

If the conservation lobby has its way, in the not-too-distant future landowners will be forced to plant trees only from native seed sources, regardless of the quality of the source from which the seeds come. There are a host of problems inherent in such a policy. For a start, our ancestors in the eighteenth century were growing oak for purposes very different from ours. Then heavily branched oaks were especially valuable, as the great boughs were ideal for ship building; equally, coppice oak, as we have already seen, was barked specifically for tanning. Now those industries have disappeared and the value of oak is in planking or veneers, for which tall, straight, clean trees are required. Are landowners to be forced to plant a genetic type of oak for which there will be no future market? As the conservation lobby is so strong that few people seem to have the guts to stand up to it, the answer is probably yes.

Regrettably, there is little prospect now that the Forestry Commission will be reformed; the likelihood is that it will continue to dominate the British forestry industry for many years to come – the last relic of a bygone age of central planning.

CHAPTER 11

Diversification

'Here's the rule for bargains: "Do other men, for they would do you." That's the true business precept.'
CHARLES DICKENS (1812-70): *Martin Chuzzlewit*

'Diversification' is the buzz word whizzing around landowning circles at the moment. In the opinion of many of the best professional brains in the business, diversification is a way of making all those high-value low-yielding assets sweat a bit. It is, in short, the Holy Grail of modern estate management. Nevertheless, landowners should beware and remember what happened to King Arthur and the Knights of the Round Table when they left Camelot and went off on the quest for the Holy Grail. The end result was the break-up of the Round Table, civil war and the collapse of King Arthur's kingdom. Holy Grails are, in short, dangerous things to look for and best left well alone.

Actually diversification is not a new game. Landowners have always indulged in it, some on a spectacular scale – like the Duke of Bridgewater, who was responsible for building most of the canal network in the latter part of the eighteenth century. Tragically the entrepreneurial streak in landowners was effectively snuffed out, between 1900 and 1980, by the burden of excessive capital and income taxes, which forced landowners to think about only one thing – survival. One of the side effects of the penal taxation regime was the removal of virtually all liquid capital out of the country and into the coffers of the Treasury. It would be interesting to work out how much money was transferred by capital taxation from the countryside for the benefit of the towns between 1900 and 1980. One thing is sure, the financial vendetta against landowners removed from them the wherewithal to carry out any entrepreneurial activities. Now, it could be argued that even if that money had been left with the landowners not all of it would have been invested on their estates. This is true, but on the whole landowners do have a tendency to invest profits made elsewhere back in their estates. In any event, the penal tax regime succeeded in destroying the historic source of rural venture capital, and much of the blame for the present dearth of rurally based businesses and the current high level of rural unemployment can be laid at the door of Lloyd George and his successors.

Diversification nowadays is like a war with lots of battle honours on offer. Some estates have avoided it all together but most have probably tried one or two of the following: deer farming, golf courses, commercial shooting, angora goats, llamas, ostriches, Christmas trees, paint-ball games, car rallying, saw mills, farm shops, pick-your-own, fishing lakes, corporate entertainment, conference centres, snail farming, crayfish, membership of Lloyd's (perhaps the most classic case of diversification) and so on *ad infinitum*. Not all of these are ill-advised and certainly some have made some people very good money, but the emphasis is on the word some – for the majority, they have proved dismal and expensive failures.

As with opening the house to the public so with diversification, it requires capital outlay and that capital might well be better employed in the stock market than in some new craze; diversification is a fashion-conscious business and at various times over the last ten years all the above have been flavour of the month. The problem is that if you set up some nice profitable fishing lakes there is no guarantee that your neighbour won't, being on the thick side, decide to do the same, thus splitting the market and driving you both into loss. The inability of most landowners to understand the basic economic rules of supply and demand is one of the serious shortcomings behind the failure of so many diversification projects.

Landowners tempted to dip their toe into the waters of diversification should remember that the penalty for failure can be the loss of the whole estate, as Lord Brocket has found at Brocket Hall. Sir Charles Wolseley discovered this harsh truth at Wolseley Hall, where an ill-thought-out venture into gardens brought to an end the family's one-thousand-year tenure of their estate, while the Philips family are now selling the palatial Luton Hoo after investing in a speculative property venture in the late 1980s boom with disastrous results. Though these are all high-profile cases, there are sadly many smaller estates and houses which have had to be sold in recent years due to their owner's desire to be 'seen to be doing something', his urge to try his hand in the glamorous world of business. Too late comes the revelation that business is not glamorous at all, that most people in it are crooks, and that the persuasive cash-flow forecast which looked so optimistic on the computer screen and promised immense riches was fatally flawed.

Landowners tempted into the murky world of commerce should never lose sight of the fact that, whereas they are taking all the risk, the professional adviser will have pocketed his fee and be many miles away should an appalling financial mess be finally revealed in all its glory, and then the only option he will have left will be to call in the estate agents.

But if one should beware of professional experts who charge one fees, how much more dangerous are one's friends, who, for a reason which totally escapes me, consider themselves qualified to advise you on every aspect of estate management though they themselves live in London and know nothing whatever about the subject. It is one of the oddities of life that if you do live in a large house everyone feels they have a right to give you advice. The fact that their expertise is minimal is not a problem to them. Personally I feel it may be because they somehow resent the fact that you are leading what seems to them an idle existence in the country while they are having to get up at seven o'clock in the morning to get into some ghastly office in the City. In any event, when they come as guests their stay is often peppered with such remarks as: 'Why don't you ...?' or, 'If I were you I would . . . ' or, 'Surely you could do . . . ' ending with, 'Oh, you are so unenterprising.'

Well, they are probably right, yet the problem with being enterprising is that there is a downside as well as an upside. The upside is that you might make quite a lot of money and be able to afford to do all the things the experts think you should do to stop the house falling down, while the downside is called losing buckets of money, which you can't afford, and eventually having to put that advertisement in *Country Life*.

Of course, you may happen to have a bucket of money. That ten-acre building plot on the outskirts of your neighbouring town might just have come good and you are now the proud possessor of that rarity, a healthy bank account. The temptations to do something 'constructive' with this windfall are all too great. If you are foolish you will consult your professional advisers. Perhaps one should not be too hard on them, poor sods; it can't be a lot of fun being a professional adviser to an impoverished estate. It is a lot more fun when there is half a million pounds or more sloshing around seeking a home. Inevitably their advice will be that you 'plough it back' into the estate. So what aspect do you 'plough it back' into?

Even if you do live within London's magic circle, or have, like some houses in the Midlands, twenty-five million people living within an hour's drive, it is a moot point whether the return on capital you might achieve by 'diversification' is really worth the effort. Before you succumb to the blandishments of your advisers, please remember that an average business investment ought to provide a minimum return of twenty per cent, but a diversification needs to produce a lot more. Why? Because you can't sell it. An ordinary business can invariably, even if it is loss-making, be flogged, but the old stable block converted at enormous expense into offices, for which suddenly there is no demand, is a white elephant. If you sell it, you create a no-go area right next door to your house – so what can you do with it?

As for the latest craze, ignore it. Little is lost in waiting to see if there really is going to be gold in golf courses (there isn't) or if angora goats produce golden fleeces (they don't) but a lot is risked by jumping on a bandwagon too quickly.

If you are still determined to risk all on a venture, try and minimise your risk by making it a joint venture. Get an experienced partner to put up the capital and run the project and in return give him a generous lease at a generous rent. Remember that landowners have got rich in the past doing exactly this – letting someone else take the risk and taking the majority of their profit in thirty or forty years when a profitable and well-run business falls neatly into their, or their son's, lap.

A significant difference between a landowner and a public company is that a landowner can (and should) take the long view while a company needs to satisfy the short-term ambitions of its shareholders and is therefore less interested in acquiring expensive freeholds and more interested in developing quick short-term profits at minimal cost. Always remember this when dealing with companies; to them a seventy-five-year lease is as good as a freehold, so give them the lease for the same money they would have paid for the freehold and leave a nice little bonus for your grandson.

The main point to remember is that you have a good reason for going into diversification – it is that you have not got enough money to satisfy your everyday needs and those of your house. Fair enough. But please consider that the reason your finances are in such a parlous state in the first place may be because you are a lousy businessman. The greatest gift a landowner can have is a knowledge of his own weaknesses.

If you are still determined to be a businessman then so be it, but why do it on your own estate? Why not start a business up in the local town or elsewhere?

When the siren voices whisper the phrase 'plough it back' into your ear, on the whole you will be wiser, and richer in the long run, if you plough it into the stock market instead. Not only will you be richer but you will find that life is a lot less hectic and you have more time to enjoy your estate – which come to think about it is what estates are meant to be for – to be enjoyed.

CHAPTER 12

Houses and Villages

Come, friendly bombs, and fall on Slough!
It isn't fit for humans now,
There isn't grass to graze a cow.
Swarm over, Death!

JOHN BETJEMAN (1906–84): *Slough*

Most estates have cottages and farmhouses scattered over them
and some even still own a whole village. For years, dwellings of
any kind were viewed as a disaster by owners. The rents they
brought in failed to cover the repairs and could not be increased
because they were 'controlled'. Indeed, until recently, it was
accepted as 'best practice' to sell off any cottage or house when
it became vacant as being more trouble than it was worth.

Rent controls were first brought in by our old friend Lloyd
George in the First World War, to protect munitions workers
who, he feared, were having their housing rents raised by
unscrupulous landlords. Gradually the legislation was extended
until the dead hand of rent control covered virtually the entire
rented-housing sector. Predictably, over time it became accepted
practice to sell off any house once it became vacant rather than
relet it and continue to lose money. In fact, such was the rate of
loss on rented property that it was generally accepted policy for
landowners to sell whole villages to the sitting tenants at knock-
down prices just to rid themselves of the long-term liability.

This is, of course, yet another instance of landowners and
their advisers making wrong decisions based on prevailing
conditions and failing to look into the future. Not that they can
be blamed, as the future, back in the 1940s and 1950s, looked
very bleak indeed and it was not until the mid-1960s that
property prices in rural England began their upward spiral.

In 1950 the average rent for one of my father's cottages in
Devon was £9.50 per annum, the agricultural wage at that time
being about £255 a year. Now the rent for one of those cottages,
under a new Assured Shorthold Tenancy, would be in the region
of £3,500 to £4,500 per annum, and the agricultural wage is
around £11,000. To put that in perspective, rents have multiplied
368 times while wages are only 43 times as high. Some may say
that the enormous rise in rents versus basic wages is evidence of
the importance of rent control. But they forget that the current
high rents are a direct result of the scarcity of rented
accommodation caused by landlords selling off housing over the
years because of rent controls. Also that the world has moved
on – for better or worse – from those days. Back in the 1950s,
regions of the United Kingdom still operated as independent
economic areas, relatively unaffected by what was happening in
the large cities and towns a hundred or so miles away. The advent
of the motorway changed all this. Suddenly it became possible for
someone working in London to jump into his car on Friday
afternoon and arrive at his weekend home in time for dinner. In
other words, house prices in the country became directly affected
by the economic performance of London rather than the local
market town ten miles away. It is a maxim of estate agents that
prices of houses are affected by three factors: location, location
and location – to which I add that location is affected by three
factors: communication, communication and communication.

So as motorways and rail networks reduce time spent travelling
between London and a property in some outlying spot in the
country, so the price of that property will go up by a certain
percentage in value for every ten minutes knocked off the journey
time.

The result of sales of cottages and houses carried out by
landowners over the years has been a chorus of protest at the
lack of cheap rural housing today. This shortage is real and few
would deny it but the reasons behind the crisis in rural housing
are a little more complex. After all, landowners more often than
not sold their houses to sitting tenants and these sitting tenants
were local people, so why is there a crisis? The unpalatable fact
is, of course, that local people then sold them on, at a great

profit, to the new breed of incomers who wished to use them as weekend cottages, retirement homes or as bases to commute from. In other words, the crisis in rural housing has been caused as much as anyone else by the local people who, pocketing their gains, moved out of the thatched cottage and into the modern bungalow of their dreams.

Talking of bungalows, some people may wonder why planners have allowed these excrescences to deface so much of England's green and pleasant land. Well many of those in the open country were built because of a loophole in the planning laws. This enjoined planning authorities to allow planning for agricultural dwellings for farmworkers and farmers. This concession to the farming community was, as ever, abused. Farmers sold their large house and then said that they had no dwelling, so were given permission to build a new one; farmers sold fifty or so acres to a third party who bought – and paid a high price – confident of getting planning for the proverbial bungalow, and so on and so forth. Not unnaturally this privilege has now been withdrawn. It is a lesson we should all have learned at school, that privileges are granted on the understanding that people are mature enough not to abuse them. If they are abused, they are rightly removed. History proves that no section of the population is ever mature enough to resist the temptation to abuse privileges when there is easy money at stake. As for the proliferation of bungalows on the outskirts of villages, no easy answer is available as to why planning was granted for them. Perhaps the easiest explanation is that planners are no different from most of the population and genuinely did not understand that they were playing a vital part in ruining the look of countless 'unspoilt' villages.

It is not only in the villages that the change in rural housing has had an impact. Outside the villages, farms have been amalgamated and farmhouses made redundant. Large pleasant family houses, described by our estate-agent friends as 'character residences', have thus been released for sale to outsiders keen to acquire a 'farmhouse with large garden and five acres, enjoying superb views over unspoilt countryside'. Incidentally quite a few buyers of such properties will approach local landowners with a view to buying another one or two acres off them for a price above the agricultural land value. Landowners should tell them to get lost and that they are no longer in the charity business. For though, on the face of it, an offer to buy an acre of land valued at say £2,000 for £5,000 may seem a good deal, remember that acre will probably add £20,000 on to the value of the buyer's property – and why should you make him a present of £15,000?

Fortunately the Conservative government finally woke up (years too late, as per normal) to the damage the various rent-control measures were doing to the private rented sector and introduced the Assured Shorthold Tenancy. This allows virtual freedom of contract between a landlord and a potential tenant and enables a landlord to repossess if the tenant is in breach of that contract. This measure has breathed new life into the rural rental sector and encouraged many landowners to rent out property which in the past they would have automatically sold on the open market. Also several owners who previously let their cottages as 'holiday lets' now rent them out to local people under Assured Shorthold Tenancies. The end result has been a small, but significant, expansion of the private rented sector in rural areas.

However, the propensity for politicians to bugger up the property market can never be overestimated. Who cares about long-term damage to the nation when important matters like short-term votes in marginal constituencies are at stake? John Major, when prime minister, certainly didn't. In 1992 he brought in the Leasehold Reform Act which effectively rewrote freely-entered-into agreements between landlords and lessees in the lessees' favour. This actually was not the first political venture into the minefield of leasehold, as Harold Wilson had already set foot there with the aim of placating Welsh miners. But in those days the reform had been limited to giving lessees the right to buy houses with a low rateable value. John Major acted to extend this right to buy to all lessees.

The immorality of retrospective legislation, changing freely-entered-into contracts between two parties in favour of one side, did not concern Mr Major. Why should it? There are relatively few landlords, while there are many tenants and lessees, all of whom have the vote. Not that it did him any good – he lost the next election by a record margin. I wonder if a single lessee voted Conservative as a thank you for all John Major had done for him. I doubt it. The common man has no sense of gratitude – and anyway a vast number of the main beneficiaries were foreigners who have made central London their home, but do not, of course, have the vote!

I make no apologies for forecasting that in twenty years or so the 1992 Leasehold Reform Act will be remembered as a disaster. The good things about leases was that they allowed a relatively good mix of people to live in central London. The leasehold system, by keeping the freehold separate, kept the cost of accommodation in central London down, and if you fancied buying the tail-end of a lease, you could afford to live in the smartest parts of London – providing you didn't mind that at the end of your lease you would have nothing.

But, back in the country, is there a solution to the permanent lack of cheap rural housing to rent? Well, there might be. The key is to encourage landowners to build cottages for rental just as their ancestors did back in the dim and distant past. One of the problems with current initiatives is that they rely on Housing Associations buying land and then developing the site. The result is that the Housing Association has to factor in the cost of the land, which might be anything from £10,000 to £20,000 a unit of accommodation. Now if landowners carried out the work themselves the land could go in at virtually zero and the only cost would be construction of the house itself at say £30,000 to 40,000 per unit. With rents of around £3,500, this could give the landlord a ten-per-cent yield, not that attractive perhaps, but if the cost of building the houses could be written off against tax over say ten years, and if business reliefs were available on capital taxation, then perhaps some landowners might be induced to dip their toes back into the waters of owning and managing private rented accommodation again, rather than just flogging off that three-acre building site to a developer to build yet more executive homes.

Another sensible solution to the housing problem is our old

friend, leasing. Say a landowner owned development land but did not have the capital available to build himself. Why, he could lease the property to developers who would build and sell the leasehold interest on. The result, because the houses were leasehold rather than freehold, would be that the houses were considerably cheaper, hence affordable. Oh, but I almost forgot – making houses affordable through leasehold is a crime today, and one must never indulge in criminal activity; so much better to make all properties so expensive that only the rich can afford them. What a bad joke our political masters are!

The sell-off of villages and redundant farmhouses has not only made living in the countryside too expensive for much of the native population, it has also fundamentally altered the character of rural communities. Many of the new arrivals bring with them urban standards and expect country people to abide by them or face the full force of civil action in the courts.

But it is not just the urban prejudices which the incomers or foreigners bring with them that are offensive, but their general attitude to the place they choose to make their home. To them they have moved to a rural idyll, but for the long established residents their village is a living, working environment. Such differing attitudes can and do create conflicts.

A further problem is the actual type of person who buys a rural property. With prices of attractive country and village properties being what they are, it is hardly surprising that most incomers are successful middle-aged professionals; their children have already grown up – so don't attend the local school; they work in the local town – so call in on the supermarket on their way home in the evening and don't buy from the village shop, and so on. In other words, they don't support the village infrastructure which is then put in danger.

The most abiding threat to villages is obviously development. The vast majority of our villages have already had their beauty ruined by insensitive development since the war. Indeed, it may be said that it is not so much the building of new houses that has caused people to loathe the concept of development but rather the type of houses that are built. It was, and still is, one of the joys of England, that on any journey of a hundred or so miles you can identify three or four different types of vernacular building. The reason is that villages were built according to what was available locally and it was not till the late nineteenth century that improvements in transport enabled bricks and slates from far away to be imported, to the detriment of the local building industries. These improvements in transport did not just destroy local building skills, they also began the long-drawn-out process of destroying the economy of the village itself. In 1911 my local village boasted a resident doctor, vet, auctioneer, schoolteacher, vicar, wheelwright, baker, blacksmith, boot maker, shopkeeper, edge-tool maker, tailor, carpenter and two pubs. Some of these trades hung on right up to the late fifties but gradually, as roads improved and car ownership spread, so the village as an economic unit serving its own immediate area saw its trade and its jobs transferred to the local market town.

What the Victorians began, the modern developer has continued, with a vengeance. Planting his ghastly little boxes across the country, regardless of local styles of architecture, intent only on securing a fat profit before moving on, he desecrates the landscape with his puerile designs.

In 1996 the Department of the Environment (DOE) unveiled a new threat to what of England remains unspoilt with its announcement that 4.4 million new houses were to be built over a twenty-five-year period from 1991. There is some mystery as to why these new homes are needed. England at present boasts a housing stock of around twenty million units of accommodation; with a total adult (over sixteen) population of forty-two million, that works out at a ratio of one house or flat for every 2.2 adults. As the population is not set to grow over the next twenty-odd years, the result of the DOE's building boom will be to reduce this ratio to under two adults for every home in England.

The supposed demand for these new houses is from the expected growth in 'single person' households caused by changing social patterns, rising divorce rate, etc. But then if this is the reason, is the countryside the best place to build the new homes? Obviously not. For a start, single people are not necessarily well off, and living in some new development in a village miles from a town means possession of a car is a necessity rather than a luxury. The obvious place to build the 4.4 million new homes is in the existing towns – and by this I do not mean on the edge of towns, I mean as near the middle of them as possible. Most British towns have been scarred over the last thirty-odd years with jerry-built low-rise office and retail developments; in London developers are buying redundant office buildings and turning them into flats – let's do the same in our county towns. If we do not follow this course of action then the future for England's towns is dire indeed. The high streets have already been badly hit by the building of out-of-town supermarkets and shopping centres; over the next dozen or so years, a revolution in the banking world is likely to lead to the closure of many branches. It is hard to see a prosperous long-term future for the county towns unless people are encouraged to return to them, and this is not as ridiculous an idea as it may seem. Living in towns – as opposed to the suburbs – has much to recommend it, especially for single people. Shops, cinemas, restaurants, pubs and even work may be within walking distance of a person's home. Also if the town centre becomes populated again then new types of shops and businesses spring up to cater for the needs of the resident population.

But the real key to rejuvenating our cities is architecture. Beautiful cities are successful cities. Ugly cities are unsuccessful. Places like Bath and Edinburgh are bursting with life and enterprise while those towns and cities which fell victim to the appalling greed of post-war developers are now struggling. It is a fact that scarcely a single building of beauty was built in the United Kingdom between 1945 and 1980, a grave indictment of Britain's developers. Big financial institutions, such as the Prudential Insurance Company – my pet hate, for putting up an excrescence of an office building in the most beautiful eighteenth-century part of Exeter – and large specialised property-investment companies, like Land Securities, fail to understand a simple fact – that if you build beautiful buildings you will be more likely to find tenants for them. That they cannot see this is one of the mysteries of the late twentieth century. The good news is that most of their buildings are so badly designed and built that few will survive far into the next century and future planners and developers will be given a superb opportunity to rectify the mistakes of their predecessors. Will they take it? I am not optimistic, but if they don't the county towns and cities of Britain will be in deeper trouble than ever in the twenty-first century.

Perhaps the most surprising aspect of the whole debate on where to build these 4.4 million new houses has been the deafening silence from the towns and cities themselves. One would have thought they would be vigorously campaigning against the building of new 'dormitory' estates on their outskirts and demanding that the housing be located in their centres. It is a frightening thing to read of the supposed housing 'need' in a particular area and then to see what an inner-city terraced Edwardian townhouse is for sale at in the same town. For instance, you can buy a Victorian terraced house in Plymouth, of the sort which in Battersea or Fulham in London would fetch several hundred thousand pounds, for around twenty-five thousand pounds, yet the dolts in the DOE still think Devon should build another ninety thousand new houses. If the demand was really so high, then surely these houses would be fetching large prices? They are not – and they won't so long as planners insist on offering a sufficient supply of detached houses in rural villages. The key to regenerating the county towns of England is to restrict development outside towns and force, I mean encourage, people to look at what is on offer within the city itself. Then, with luck, a 'halo effect' will be achieved, as has happened in so much of London – i.e. as people do up terraced housing so others move in to follow suite, then restaurants and shops begin to open to cater for the demand of the comparatively affluent owners of the properties and so on.

The above is, of course, all commonsense; it is a pity the DOE has so little of it – but then one must remember that the House Builders' Federation is a particularly powerful lobby; politicians should recall, when listening to their blandishments, that no single organisation has been responsible for ruining more acres of land, destroying more villages or wrecking more town centres than the membership of this particular – supposedly benevolent – organisation.

The reaction of the House Builders' Federation to the uproar caused by the announcement of the proposal to build the 4.4 million new homes was predictable. A Mr Humber, the director of the HBF, made a speech in 1996 to the Town and Country Planning Association (that is not a joke, there actually is one!) from which I cannot resist quoting the odd gem. For instance, on building in towns and cities he said: 'We cannot turn them into dustbins for the shire county NIMBYs.' Now, in my ignorance, I thought he wanted to turn great areas of the countryside into 'dustbins' for those from the towns! But perhaps, in common with many modern men, his grasp of English is not all that it might be. He then went on: 'If the cities become yet more overcrowded, if education gets worse, as does traffic and crime, if the quality of life declines, then more people will try to leave and put pressure on the countryside.' Actually his argument is rubbish. Sadly most cities are not crowded and that is what is wrong with them. Walk round the centre of most county towns at ten o'clock at night and they are empty, there is no buzz, no restaurants are open, no late-night shops are to be found; the simple reason is that no one lives in them any more – the members of the Town and Country Planning Association have seen to that and turned most towns and cities into deserts at night.

If the HBF got its way and was allowed to build willy-nilly over greenfield sites, this would result in the cities declining still further and crime would rise, education standards fall and the general quality of life deteriorate, because the prosperous and intelligent middle classes would sell up and move to one of Mr Humber's members' ghastly little boxes in the country (although you can hardly call living in a hundred-acre new town 'country') leaving behind all who couldn't afford to move.

A last quote from Mr Humber, this time complaining about high-density housing being built in London's docklands: ' . . . they are in some cases building tiny houses, which can only be the slums of the future, on sites which should, at best, be used for road widening or to provide open space'. Really, now I wonder if Mr Humber and the members of the Town and Country Planning Association ought not to take a trip to Chelsea or Kensington or Mayfair and see how valuable small houses in narrow streets can be and how desirable such areas are to live in. But then, given half a chance, he and his friends would undoubtedly sweep all that away for 'road widening' and to provide 'open spaces'; after all, presumably it was past and, I suspect, a few present members of the Town and Country Planning Association who filled the poisoned chalice with tower blocks and the like!

House builders love 'greenfield sites', not just because they are easy to work but because of an anomaly in the taxation rules. No VAT is levied on new houses, but if a builder converts a disused office building or old warehouse into living accommodation or refurbishes an existing block of flats he has to pay VAT on all his outgoings. Paradoxically, this discourages builders from doing just what the public want them to do. The simple solution is to zero rate refurbishments as well as new houses, but VAT is a complex tax and, because we are forced to give a percentage of the total VAT raised every year to the European Union (so they can give it to the Irish or the Greeks) any change in VAT has to be authorised by the European Union.

Britain has so far escaped having to charge VAT on new housing as it has pretended that new housing is necessary for reasons of 'social policy'; so now you know that those expensive executives homes with double garages being built on the edge of your village are 'social housing'! Unfortunately there is little likelihood of the European Union agreeing to allow us to zero rate refurbishments and renovations as, once a VAT rate is established, EU law decrees it can never be reduced. The alternative solution would be to impose VAT at the full rate on new houses built on greenfield sites. Such a policy would elicit howls of rage from house builders who would make sure the purchaser bore the increased cost.

While on the face of it this looks a logical response, it is Mickey Mouse economics. The imposition of VAT on new homes would not make an iota of difference to the price of the new home. Why? Because builders already sell their houses for the maximum amount they think they can get away with; *ergo* if they had to pay 17.5% on the cost of building the property they could not pass it on as no one would buy the thing at that price.

So what would happen? Well builders would initially have to absorb the extra cost of the tax, but in the future they would factor it into their calculations when buying building land – in other words, they would pay less for development land to enable them to continue to keep their current profit margins on future developments. The only loser would therefore be the landowner, who instead of getting, say, £400,000 an acre, would only get £300,000

So now you know why there are 800,000 empty homes in the UK at present, and why no one is that keen on renovating the old warehouses and redundant office buildings which are such a feature of so many of our towns and cities. It is all the fault of our friendly European Union.

CHAPTER 13

The Family

The ownership of land is a partnership not only between
those who are living, but between those who are living,
those who are dead, and those who are yet to be born.

EDMUND BURKE (1729–97)

If the visible side of an estate is a large house and extensive park
then the invisible element is the people, whose presence make
the whole thing work and without whom it would be just
another dead museum.

First and foremost must be the owner and his immediate
family. Whether the estate and house sinks or swims depends
totally on them and their aims and ambitions – or lack of them,
as the case may be. Because, as we have seen, a lack of ambition
and enterprise can sometimes have a far more positive effect on
the financial health of an estate than an all-singing, all-dancing
entrepreneurial approach.

This has always been true of estates; many in the past were
beggared and eventually broken up by foolish attempts to
finance an owner's ambitions at court, in Parliament, or even in
entertaining monarchs such as Edward VII.

Sometimes I feel that estate owners lose sight of what is the
most important department on their estate. It is not the home
farm or the forestry or the house opening, it is their own family.

It follows from that that the most important decision one has
to make in one's life is whom to marry. The rightness of the
decision is not only a matter of concern for fellow members of
the landed gentry and nobility but for one's whole estate. The
future of the estate could be threatened if the girl comes from
bad breeding stock and is going to produce thick, idle
spendthrifts, wastrels or gamblers, or maybe a mixture of the

lot, or even, perish the thought, a queer, which will effectively mean the end of your line. So breeding is vital and parents and grandparents of potential spouses should be carefully examined for the sort of faults you do not want in either your wife or your children.

Another quality to look for is thrift. To most house owners the sad truth is that economy is vital for survival. Extravagance in a wife is something which few estates can long afford, especially if it is directed at completely useless things like expensive designer clothes and hairdressing. Wives who hanker after the bright lights of London should on all accounts be avoided like the plague; although the streets of London may be paved in gold, it is only so for those who run shops and restaurants and the like and not for the people who trudge up and down them.

A good test for a girl is to introduce her to your black labrador as soon as possible in your courtship. A girl's reaction to being greeted by a wet muddy dog while still in her smart London clothes is generally an infallible pointer to her suitability for the post of chatelaine. If she screams with horror, throws up her hands in disgust and later complains volubly about the dog sharing your bed, then you know that you have got a wrong 'un and you ought to disentangle yourself fast.

But, of course, the main thing is that the two of you must be compatible; you will probably never be completely so as a woman's brain is radically different from a man's and her ideas of what is important can sometimes drive even the most long-suffering man to the outer limits of exasperation. I always found the most trying time in my marriage was when my wife was pregnant and spent endless, laborious hours trying to get the house spotless, only for me and my dog to walk into the kitchen in muddy boots in search of a mid-morning cup of coffee. Pregnancy for a man is a very trying time indeed and it is hard always to be totally understanding. However, if you are more or less compatible you may avoid a highly expensive and messy divorce some years later.

Once you are married and have moved into your big house it is probable that your new spouse will put pressure on you to indulge in that most expensive of hobbies, interior decoration.

Don't panic. Instead, agree with everything proposed but insist that you have the opportunity to view materials – wallpapers, paint samples, etc. – and play for time. Time is vital. Initially the paintwork and carpets may have appeared to your wife a touch on the grubby side – hardly surprising as they date from fifty years ago. But, given time, they will begin to exert their own peculiar charm on her and, if you can persuade your friends and, more importantly, some of hers, to say, 'Oh, you are so clever not to have destroyed the charm of the house by wallpapering everything!' or, 'I just love this faded look, I do think it's so romantic. Promise me you won't ruin my favourite room by painting it!' You are in with more than half a chance of keeping things as they were.

Your main enemy is your wife's friends, especially those with a 'business interest' in interior decorating; as virtually every other girl one meets nowadays seems to be involved in interior decorating in some form or fashion, it is odds-on that your wife will have a number of these as friends. Try and keep them away from the house if possible for as long as you can. This will be difficult as they will want to come down and poke their noses around, and give 'free' advice in the hope of picking up some lucrative and prestigious business. The key, of course, is to get your wife pregnant and give her a large family as soon as possible, then she will be too busy looking after the children to think of decorating rooms and you can relax.

It cannot be overstressed that divorce is the one thing that should be avoided at all costs. It is very expensive, the lawyers both sides employ charge the earth and are totally unscrupulous in acting 'in the best interests' of their client. Incidentally whenever a lawyer says this please remember he is acting in *his* best interests. Divorce is an extremely stressful process for both parties and when your lawyer says smoothly: 'Just leave it to me and let me take care of it . . .' it is all too easy weakly to agree and let them get on with it – DON'T. Why? Because he will write a stiff letter to his opposite number who will gleefully show it to his client who will then go ballistic and authorise his or her lawyer to unleash the full barrage back. In all likelihood the two lawyers will later have a friendly chat on the telephone and agree they have got a really good little money earner here.

It goes without saying that divorce is not good for your children, and if the most important person on an estate is the present owner then surely the second most important one is his heir. Once again, many people seem to forget this and neglect to bring up their children properly. Time spent rolling around on the floor with your planned successor is not wasted but is, you may be sure, a solid investment in the future. The Jesuits used to boast that a child given to them before the age of seven was theirs for life, and as you have yours from the start, there shouldn't be a problem; sadly there often is.

It is vital you ensure that your offspring from the earliest age take on board your prejudices. I well remember my governess explaining communism to me when I was about five years old. She did it quite brilliantly. 'If the communists ever ruled,' she said, 'then Panda [my number one teddy bear] would be taken away from you and shared out among the local children.' Such simple explanations are easy for a child to understand and will make an indelible impression on them. For myself, when my children ask for an ice cream I often say that 'sadly Daddy has got no money'. When they ask why, I answer: 'Because Mummy has gone and spent all the money on plants for the garden.' Mummy then gets a lot of rather undeserved stick but I hope that the message, that if you spend money on one thing you can't have another, lodges somewhere in their brains.

As they grow older, so they should be introduced to the problems of estate management, encouraged to go out with the gamekeeper, taken into the woods, as I was by my father, to prune trees and so forth – in other words, not allowed to fester in some centrally heated room playing infantile games on a computer.

When they leave school the question of careers raises its ugly head. This is a difficult one. What to do with your son and heir while he is waiting for you to die. If he is clever, bright and hard working then you have, by luck (or good selection?), scooped the pool and he will probably have no problem getting a well-paid job in the city and may even – as a surprisingly large number of sons of landowners have in recent years – make a fortune. The difficulty is if he is not very bright and is totally unfitted for any form of job. Even that old fall-back the armed forces has introduced a nasty two-day series of tests and interviews which are rather hard, as I found out, to pass.

As for the City, that too has changed and no longer can a well-placed telephone call ensure your offspring a job in some merchant bank. Strangely, as merchant banks and stockbrokers have become more meritocratic in their employment policy so they have lost their independence and been beset by scandals; perhaps the old ways were not so bad after all?

In recent years it has become fashionable to punt the eldest son off to the Royal Agricultural College at Cirencester to learn the ropes of estate management prior to his taking over control from his aged father. The concept is praiseworthy – though, as is so often the case with concepts, the results do not always live up to the expectations. When you think about it, the reasons are fairly obvious. On the whole, an heir punted off to Cirencester is not over-blessed with brains and it is the final solution of exasperated parents who have finally given up on any chance of getting him a 'proper' job. Parents of heirs to estates are no different from any other parents and dislike intensely having to answer queries from 'concerned' friends which go something like this:

'And what is Johnny up to now?'

'Oh, well, he is at home at present, the job in the City didn't really suit him you know.'

'Oh, poor you, it must be such a worry for you both. Now Charlie's doing very well at Rumbolds and . . . '

After a bit even the most long-suffering parent loses patience and gives the heir a one-way ticket to Cirencester. The danger of such a policy is that on his return he may actually want to manage the estate in a 'hands on' fashion and, as that was supposed to be the reason you sent him on the course in the first place, it is rather hard to deny him the opportunity of showing what he can do.

Some, of course, succeed admirably, but others, convinced that their qualification gives them the equivalent of wings, try to fly and, after spending inordinate amounts of capital, fall to earth with a resounding crash. This can be particularly irritating if you have 'made over' a large chunk of the estate to him, in order to avoid Inheritance Tax, only to see him squander the lot on some stupid project. Because you have to live seven years after making over property to your son for it to be free of tax on your death, the property is sometimes made over too soon; many a parent gnashes his teeth as helplessly he watches his son squander his patrimony.

Since earliest times, landowners have had to find ways of protecting their estates from spendthrift heirs. Over the centuries various legal means were tried and tested in order to ensure that estates were not dissipated or left away from the family. Most of these forms of 'entailment' fell down because Common Law does not recognise the creation of a settlement which seeks to secure property in perpetuity and the law gradually evolved whereby any trust or settlement which tried to tie up an estate for longer than the 'lives of people in being and twenty-one years beyond' was void. However, man's ingenuity being inexhaustible, a way was found round this problem by means of something called a 'strict settlement'. This, in essence, meant a landowner agreed to settle his estates on his eldest son and on his, yet to be born, eldest grandson. It was renewed on his son's marriage who, because he was dependant on his father for necessary allowances in order to live, readily agreed to enter into a renewal of the settlement – thus effectively perpetuating the entail.

However these forms of entail were eroded by the passage of Lord Cairn's Settled Land Act of 1882 which allowed holders of entailed estates to sell upon notice to the trustees. While I suspect many landowners welcomed the measure when it was introduced, the long-term consequences were disastrous as it allowed the Treasury vultures to assess such estates for death-duty purposes as freehold rather than only as a life interest. The many break-ups of estates since then owe much to this act and to the fact that modern landowners can, and do, use their estates as collateral when entering into business ventures. Previously, under the entailment system, an owner only had a life interest and therefore could not borrow money on the freehold value of the property. So if debts became an embarrassment the creditors could not seize the estate and sell it. My own situation is a classic example. In 1863 my ancestor had accumulated debts of over £60,000 and had to flee the country to escape his creditors, but the creditors could not appropriate any assets to sell, apart from renewable ones like timber. Thus estates could survive the most profligate owners.

If your eldest son is a problem, what of the rest of your brood? You must pray – as I do constantly – that they are blessed by brains and ability and will be able to make their way in the world, otherwise the future is indeed bleak. It has to be said that the average landowner's breeding line does not afford grounds for optimism. It is unlikely that you yourself have ever held down a highly remunerative job, let alone any of your ancestors. If your other children turn out as hopeless as you and your father probably were then you have a decided problem. For a start your wife is likely to put pressure on you to make some sort of 'provision' for them. This is tempting but should be resisted as it is unlikely the estate is large enough to have big slices cut off it to subsidise the laziness and stupidity inherent in your younger offspring, especially if such traits have already manifested themselves in your eldest boy. At such time you should remember the rule: 'Give as you received.' In other words if you were left the whole estate because you were the eldest and your sisters and brothers were left go hang then it is not for you to decide that this time you ought to do something different. In short, you should abide by the rule of primogeniture; after all, if previous generations had not rigidly followed it it is highly unlikely you would have any estate left in the first place. If, on the other hand, you have, by your own efforts, built up a substantial pile of cash, why then it is up to you how you dispose of it.

Finally, of course, and most importantly, the father must know when to go. Too many owners hang on for too long. It is sadly all too common to see an old couple rattling around in a great big house while their son, married now with three children, camps in a farmhouse somewhere on the estate. This is a recipe for strife. Big houses are designed for children and if the grandchildren are not brought up in it they will probably end up loathing the bloody place. For children, big houses are just fun: they can bicycle up the passages and round the great hall, run riot upstairs and amuse themselves for hours. They also have one enormous advantage over adults – they don't feel the cold.

Not only will the children enjoy the big house, your son and daughter-in-law are probably longing to get their hands on it. If you do decide to move out you must raise no objection when panelling you painted white at great expense is stripped and returned to its bare wood, Victorian decorative schemes, considered the height of vulgarity in the 1950s and 1960s and papered over to universal acclaim, are once again exposed to the light of day, and so on. Remember this is but a short episode in the history of the house and daughters-in-law have been behaving thus for centuries. If you deny your son and his wife their opportunity now, they will spend their money and time on doing up the farmhouse and when the moment does come for them to move into the big house they will quite possibly turn round and say, 'No, thanks, we are quite happy where we are.'

Why do so many owners selfishly refuse to move out of their houses and deny their grandchildren the joys of growing up in one? I don't know – it baffles me. I can't wait to hand the front-door keys over to my eldest son and retire to a 'sunset home' somewhere on the estate, where I can experience the joys of modern convenience living without worrying about the cost.

CHAPTER 14

The Professionals

'. . . let's kill all the lawyers.'

SHAKESPEARE: *Henry VI, Part 2*

Running an estate has always been a complex business and is becoming more and more so; it is therefore hardly surprising that professional advisers have come to feature prominently in the lives of most owners.

It is strangely perplexing that though today's stately-home owner is almost invariably chronically short of cash himself, he should give large amounts to such undeserving causes as professional advisers. But then he has little choice in the matter. Even with the relatively benign taxation system of today, a landowner spends an inordinate amount of time, energy and money planning his death. In order for the estate and house to survive it is essential he gets his tax planning right, for if he fails, the estate will, to all intents and purposes, be forfeited to the Treasury. It has sometimes seemed to me that if capital taxes were abolished the loss to the Treasury would be comparatively small (Inheritance Tax and Capital Gains Tax only yield £2.5 billion per annum or around 1% of total taxation) but the gain to the country as a whole would be enormous as all the brain power which is at present dedicated to avoiding such taxes would be freed up and put to some more constructive use.

So who are these professionals and how do they fit into the picture? The short answer is they are symbiotic parasites – we need them and they need us. They are the solicitors, accountants and land agents without whom no estate could function, and who, like anyone else, need feeding and clothing. As in the natural world, however, there are different types of parasite. Some are beneficial to the species others can destroy it.

The fatter the parasite the more it needs to feed, and in country-estate terms there are some pretty fat parasites out there.

Most, perhaps inevitably, are based in London. Estate owners are after all no different from ordinary mankind and are as divided into wise and foolish virgins as any other group of people. Some are impressed by deep-pile carpets, swanky West End offices, smooth young men and portly partners. Perhaps it is fear which causes owners to go through the portals of such establishments? Fear of losing out because one has not got the BEST advice. I think that must be the reason and it is not one without merit. More estates have probably been killed by bad professional advice than any other single factor – agricultural depressions, confiscatory taxation, even wayward offspring, all might have been coped with, but bad, even in some cases, dishonest, professional advice has been a killer. And it is certainly the case that the vast majority of estates, right up to the late 1960s and early 1970s, were run and managed by local firms of solicitors. Many of these firms proved themselves grossly incompetent, if not actually dishonest – hence presumably the rush to London lawyers.

Whatever the reason for changing to top London firms, it certainly is not economy. For as your feet sink into the carpet and the pretty secretary ushers you into a grandiose office for a quiet chat with the senior partner, prior to a light designer lunch, it is worth remembering who is paying for all this – you!

Like leeches they cling on to your account, sucking the life blood from your still living body in the form of indecently fat fees, and incredibly, people happily pay! It staggers me – especially as the rapacity of lawyers is hardly a new phenomenon. Writing in the late eighteenth century, a landowner in Lancashire, Nicholas Blundell, advised his heir 'to show diligence in taking some care of your own concerns, for when concerns of the moment are left to stewards and attorneys, they grow rich by their master's poverty'.

Alternatively, of course, you can employ local firms of solicitors, accountants and land agents, pay reasonable fees and enjoy a good working relationship with people who have your best interests at heart. Local firms today are a very different breed from those that existed in the pre-war and immediate post-war period; now you are likely to find standards are as high among the professionals in your county town as in the grandest London firm. And, after all, if there is a particularly difficult tax or legal problem, you can always wander up to London and pay for top advice, but it is fairly stupid to pay serious money for advice and management from London all the time.

Perhaps the worst form of parasite of all is the 'professional trustee'. Do you hate your heir? Then put his inheritance into a trust managed by London-based trustees. Did your father hate you or was he just plain thick? It has got to be one or other of these reasons, otherwise he would not have saddled the estate with these pariahs. These people have nothing whatever to recommend them – they are not clever, they probably do not even buy you a decent lunch, but they sure know how to type out the fee bills.

Here are some tips for dealing with these dregs of humanity if you are unfortunate enough to be afflicted with them. First, challenge their bills and demand to see all past bills going back say, six years. I guarantee that if you take this line and make sufficient fuss you will recover around ten per cent, or more, of fees paid over the period. Second, buy a basic law book and examine in minute detail how they have managed your affairs – you never know, you may be able to sue them for negligence. Thirdly, buy yourself one of those chess clocks, the ones which only start ticking when you press the button and then stop when you press it again – never attend a meeting without one. Place it ostentatiously on the desk in front of your trustees and only start it when they stop exchanging pleasantries.

In other words attack. And don't feel bad about hurting the feelings of that charming old gentleman across the desk – remember he's only in it for the money and has been ripping you and your family off for years. Sadly it is virtually impossible to sack these blood suckers, and why should they resign from a nice little earner? The scenario gets worse if, as well as being your trustees, they are also executors of your father's will, because the fee bill is based not solely on the amount of work required to wind the estate up, but also on a percentage of the value of the estate! This is a scandalous case of 'having your cake and eating it'. Regardless of the amount of work carried out the executors are guaranteed a fat fee and – in addition – have the gall to charge extra fees for their time!

Be this all as it may, trustees are an integral feature of most estates, so if one discards the professionals to whom does one turn to fill this role? The obvious answer is friends who have had similar problems and have a knowledge of running estates and are happy to take on the job out of their friendship for you and their love of the estate. If you are appointing trustees for your son, then try and find people who are between your own age and his. But the most important thing is to ensure that they have the same aims and ambitions for the estate as you have and, in the event of your untimely death, will ensure that the management strives for continuity.

If you are saddled with professional trustees and want to get rid of them I am afraid it is probably going to cost you money. They are not going to resign meekly from a nice little earner which brings them in regular fat fees without a bribe.

Moving on from these parasites, we encounter another group of professionals, the vultures. They hang about, eyeing you as you crawl over the desert trying desperately to survive long enough for the aged relation to drop off his or her perch and leave you the long-hoped-for legacy which will solve your financial problems. These vultures, unlike the real birds, are on the whole charming and friendly people who do you no harm and can normally be relied on to give you lots of good lunches. A prime examples of vultures are the large auction houses. It is their job to know as much about you and your current finances as possible, so when Great Aunt Agatha finally does hop the twig, leaving her entire worldly goods to the cats' home, they are there with soothing words and a damp flannel to dab your brow, all geared up to sell your pictures for you. There is the oft-told tale of how some years ago the chairmen of Sotheby's and Christie's were together at the funeral of a noted collector when suddenly the chairman of Christie's noticed that his opposite number, Peter Wilson of Sotheby's, had slipped away; he was already in the house cataloguing the collection for auction!

It is axiomatic in landowning circles that almost the first action of an heir when he takes possession of his inheritance is to sack the entire collection of his father's professional advisers and start again. This happens particularly when Daddy has hung on to the reins of power for rather too long and the heir has had to sit on the sidelines gnashing his teeth in fury as he witnesses the professionals racking up the fee bills. Only the other day a friend of mine innocently asked me if I was familiar with 'notional rents'. I cudgelled my brain but could not think what on earth they were and had to ask for an explanation. He was equally puzzled by my ignorance as he was under the impression that they were common to all estates which paid their firm of agents on a percentage of the rental income. It appears, for those of you still wondering, that notional rents are assessed by some agents on houses which are part of the estate but for which, for some reason, no rent is charged, e.g. those housing estate pensioners or employees. The agent will argue that as he is responsible for managing the property he ought to receive a fee for the work, which sounds on the face of it fair, although most landowners would regard this as rather 'hot practice'. In this particular case it is jam today but not jam tomorrow for one unscrupulous firm, as when my friend finally takes over they will get their marching orders extremely quickly.

Observing the antics of many firms one is forced to conclude that 'jam today' is their priority. As an owner gets older he will delegate more and more to these firms and become more and more out of touch with reality. Then it is that the professional comes into his own and makes hay while the heir can do little but writhe in frustration, vowing vengeance when the time comes for the reins of power to fall into his hands.

Some landowners, especially those who have completed the proverbial course at Cirencester, feel that they are eminently qualified to act as agents on their own estate, thus saving the fees. Personally, I would advise against this as it will mean dealing directly with your tenants, people whom you have probably grown up with, perhaps even attended the village school with in early childhood, and arguing with them about rents, repairs and suchlike, i.e. about money, will not be easy.

Most gentlemen are not very good at negotiations when money is at stake, especially when the end result of success will be to remove cash from tenants' pockets and put it into their own. Even people who are as hard as steel and brilliantly successful in negotiations on behalf of third parties quite often find that they are routinely taken to the cleaners when it comes to dealing on their own account.

On balance, few landowners will be worse off for paying an agent to handle the vast majority of estate negotiations, and most will be considerably richer. Among the advantages is the obvious one – that an agent acting for you, or even better for your trustees, can never be put in a corner by a tenant. He can always use the get-out option of having to 'discuss this with his principle'. It is *de rigeur*, in whatever negotiations you are engaged upon, to have such an option open to you at all times.

CHAPTER 15

Field Sports

'Unting is the sport of kings, the image of war
without its gilt, and only five and twenty per cent of
its danger.'

SURTEES (1805-64): *Handley Cross*

It is impossible to write a book about the countryside of the
United Kingdom without devoting at least a chapter to field
sports. Most of the books ignore the subject entirely, but this
may be because they are on the whole written by ignorant
pseudo-environmentalists, who know little if anything about the
subject they purport to be expert on.

To understand how positive have been the effects of field
sports on the country over recent centuries it is necessary to ask
what the countryside would look like today if landowners had
not so often loved to hunt, shoot and fish. How would the
appearance of rural England differ if we had behaved in the
manner of effete continental aristocrats and sponsored ballets
and operas instead of spending our money riding to hounds,
shooting and fishing? Well, there is no doubt the landscape and
wildlife of the countryside would be very different.

For a start it is doubtful whether the fox would have survived
as part of our native fauna without the support of the hunt. Back
in the nineteenth century there was such a dearth of foxes that
they were imported from France and Germany and sold in
Leadenhall market where they could be bought for around
fifteen shillings a head! The reason for the shortage had little to
do with the numbers being killed by hunts but far more to do
with the fact that most people in the country kept poultry, and
foxes are, to say the least, partial to chickens, geese and ducks.
Such was the virulence of the campaign waged against foxes,

many parishes offering a bounty on the head of any fox brought in dead, that they would certainly have been eradicated from great swathes of the United Kingdom but for the sudden popularity of hunting.

At the same time those who hunted realised the necessity of planting copses and woods in which foxes could make their earths, so hunting not only saved the fox from possible extinction but also helped form the English landscape. Likewise the red deer on Exmoor were on the verge of extinction and were only saved by the advent of stag hunting.

As with hunting so with shooting. The red grouse has done more to protect the heather-clad hills of Scotland, and parts of England and Wales, from the ravages of overstocking with sheep or planting inappropriately with trees, than any government-sponsored initiative and at no cost to the taxpayer. The great enthusiasm for pheasant shooting in the nineteenth century caused many woods to be planted. As early as 1837, Lawrence Rawstrone could write in his book *Gamonia*: 'There has risen of late years a great rage for planting, not only from that spirit of improvement which has displayed itself in adorning the mansions of the rich, but from the introduction of *battues*, which require extensive preserves and numerous coverts.' Interestingly the author then goes on to deplore the modern (1837!) desire for big bags, giving as an example: 'It is a thing scarcely to be credited by our forefathers that two shots should kill in one day three hundred and fifty pheasants, which was done a few years ago at Comme in Worcestershire.'

It is also doubtful in the extreme whether our rivers would have survived in anything like their present-day form without the constant vigilance of fishermen, or indeed whether the Atlantic salmon would have survived at all. Back in 1896 our rivers were in an appalling state, a mixture of uncontrolled commercial netting and industrial pollution having wrought havoc. The Tyne was virtually empty of fish, having been plundered by netsmen to the tune of over a hundred and twenty thousand fish a year until only twenty years before. Everywhere in England and Wales the story was same – a disaster threatened. That it was averted, the decline in salmon numbers reversed and rivers restored to health, was principally the result of pressure put on the authorities by the riparian community.

Today the salmon is once more threatened, and once again the leading spirits behind the attempts to safeguard it are among the ranks of the fishermen; not only fishermen from these shores either, for the man who has probably done more than any other to safeguard the future of the salmon is Orri Vigfusson, who has lead a highly successful campaign to buy off the sea-fishing fleets who were plundering salmon from their feeding grounds. It is true that there is a government body – the National Environment Agency – which has notional responsibility for the health of the nation's rivers but no fisherman rates them highly or expects much from them. Owners and fishermen everywhere know that their rivers will flourish or fade away by their efforts or lack of them. Evidence of this is a movement of interested parties to form associations dedicated to restoring single-river systems.

And so it goes on. A sportsman by definition does not want to eliminate his quarry but to harvest the surplus. He wants to improve its habitat so it can breed more effectively, and as what is good for game birds is also good for a large number of other species, they too benefit.

Of course, many people abhor all field sports because they think they are cruel. Indeed, the revered National Trust has recently published a lengthy scientific report supporting allegations that stag-hunting is traumatic for the quarry. It has banned stag-hunting on its land on Exmoor and in the Quantocks, in defiance of the stated wishes of Sir Richard Acland, the donor of the majority of its Exmoor estate. At the risk of repeating myself, I suggest the National Trust should change its name. If I trust someone, I depend on them to keep their word, without bothering with all the tedious legal niceties which fill our legal friends' pockets at little or no benefit to anyone else. Sadly that is what Sir Richard did – he had faith in the organisation. Be warned! From now on remember – you can't trust the National Trust.

Incidentally I would like to take issue on whether hunting – be it of stags or foxes – is really 'cruel'. Of course, not being either a fox or a stag I appreciate that my opinions might be considered valueless; however, having once been 'hunted' by an elephant in Zimbabwe, I know what it is like to run away from a sodding great lump of flesh whose sole ambition in life is to kill you.

It happened like this. A chap called Peter Croft, of the *Shooting Times*, and I were writing a story on big game in Zimbabwe and we were out in the bush with a hunter and a couple of trackers looking for a rhino; instead, we came across a herd of nine cow elephants. All was quiet and we observed them for some minutes; presently they started to move off so we began to walk back to where our truck was – half a mile or so away. Suddenly, for no apparent reason, the herd swung right handed so they were in extended line and then, from a distance of perhaps two hundred and fifty yards, flapped their ears, raised their trunks and came for us.

At first I was relatively relaxed – after all, we had a hunter with us. But that feeling of calm fled in a moment as I saw our black trackers disappear at the double and heard the hunter shout 'Run!' Our guide fired shots over the heads of the elephants to scare them off but a few kept coming. Our running was chaotic; both Peter and I stumbled and fell, then got up and plunged on. We came to a fork in a path; I decided to go left while Peter Croft and our hunter went right.

Next moment I fell headlong. I looked round. An elephant was twenty yards away; it put its head down and began to charge. I was dead. From deep in my head I heard a voice say: 'Elephants like to kneel on you – role into a ball and keep your eyes open, and when you see the knees come down, roll out of the bloody way.' A second later the blue sky was blotted out by a mass of grey flesh. The elephant played its part to perfection. It tried to kneel on me. Every time I saw those knees coming down I rolled – and screamed like hell all the time.

Eventually, after what seemed an age, the sky above me cleared and was blue once again. I looked up. My elephant had backed off some forty or fifty yards and was looking at me quizzically. I got up and gave her a slight bow and she, turning, trotted off to rejoin her herd.

The point of the story is that I never, except for a brief

moment, felt fear. I never lost the belief – however impossible the situation seemed – that I would somehow get out of that situation alive. To prove the point I lit a cigarette afterwards and my hands did not shake. Yet I dare say that if I had been killed, and the good professor who wrote the National Trust report had dissected me, he would have found ample evidence of stress and drawn the erroneous conclusion that I was petrified out of my wits. What goes for me, I argue, may surely apply to wild animals as well. If you think, well it's all right for him, he is probably very brave, then you are wrong on two counts – first, bravery is the overcoming of fear and not lack of fear itself; second, I have been bloody frightened on several occasions in my life and certainly do not consider myself 'brave'.

There is something else which the good professor seems to have discounted – possibly because being a townee he knows no better. The best test of whether the way you have killed an animal is cruel is in the taste of the meat. Fear in animals translates itself into 'taint' in the meat, which effectively makes it inedible. Stags which are hunted are shot by the huntsman – not torn to pieces by hounds as mythology has it – and are later sold for venison, which is eminently edible. If, on the other hand, one comes across a deer which has been caught in a barbed-wire fence for many hours and has struggled in vain to free itself, and one shoots it and tries to eat the flesh, it is inedible.

Field sports, especially hunting, are often criticised for the ritualistic approach to the killing of the prey; yet little is said or done about the nauseating ritual killing of sheep and goats by halal and kosher butchers on behalf of Muslim and Jewish communities – I wonder why not?

Finally, it is worth remembering that many of those who are against field sports, unwittingly harbour the cruellest killer of all – the domestic cat. It is estimated that the cat population of the UK kills annually some eighty-two million birds! And cats do not just kill, they enjoy playing with their prey and teasing it before they kill it. Anyone who has witnessed a cat doing this will realise that for sheer cruelty the cat has no equal, yet, as far as I know, no one – not the RSPCA, nor the RSPB nor the National

Trust, let alone the League Against Cruel Sports – has suggested that all domestic cats should be destroyed. Why? A silly question because we all know the answer, a large number of their supporters own cats. It is the hypocrisy of groups such as these that annoys countrymen as much as anything else

This brings us back to shooting and its beneficial effect on wildlife and the environment. I seem to hear mounting cries from the RSPB brigade about keepers persecuting anything with a hooked beak. Now that was certainly true of old-style keepering. But I wonder if the RSPB's cries are not a little like the pot calling the kettle black, for while old-fashioned keepers may have favoured game birds to hawks, now the RSPB favours hawks over all other species of bird. In short, it carries out what seems to me to be a fascist policy of refusing to admit that hawks need, like any predator, to be controlled. I sometimes wonder how a body can continue to call itself the Royal Society for the Protection of Birds when many of the species which it nurtures live by killing – often rather gruesomely – other birds! How would you like to be plucked alive?

Actually, of course, the RSPB does support the culling of predators – but only if they do *not* have hooked beaks. Thus it will, in some of its reserves, sanction the killing of magpies and crows. This to my mind is a racialist policy – is it, I wonder, anything to do with these birds being mainly coloured black? Heaven forbid. But if you allow magpies and crows to be controlled, why not sparrowhawks, hen harriers and the like? The RSPB policy is short on logic and long on emotion and public relations.

Even when the RSPB is provided with independent scientific evidence showing the damage done by an uncontrolled raptor population it still refuses to admit that there may be a case for allowing the control of hawks. For five years researchers from the Game Conservancy Trust and the Institute of Terrestrial Ecology (part of the National Environment Research Council) carried out a detailed study of the effect of hen harriers on a grouse moor belonging to the Duke of Buccleuch. Their report was published in 1997.

The findings were damning. Over the period of the study, the number of hen harriers on the moor increased from two to fourteen breeding females and the number of breeding female peregrines from three to six. During the last two years of the study, when bird-of-prey numbers were at their peak, hawks killed about thirty per cent of overwintering grouse and a further thirty per cent of the potential breeding stock in the spring, and then finished off by killing around thirty-seven per cent of the grouse chicks. The end result was that a moor which in the past could produce, in a good year, annual bags of around two thousand brace was reduced to recording a bag of only a hundred brace in 1996.

One of the great ironies of the debate over hen harriers – which the RSPB refuses to recognise – is that hen harriers, as ground-nesting birds, benefit from keepered moors. Hen harriers can, in effect, only flourish at such densities as they achieved on the Langholm Moor because the gamekeepers control potential nest predators, such as foxes. In other words, the logical long-term effect of the RSPB's refusal to contemplate any form of control of hen harriers is that the hen-harrier population will itself decline!

As the result of such levels of predation as occurred at Langholm most owners would eventually give up the moor in disgust – sack the keepers, stop conserving the heather and let 'nature' take its course – and in twenty year's time the area of heather would have declined substantially, if not totally disappeared, and so would the hen harrier; but try explaining such an obvious scenario to the RSPB and you will be met with blank moronic stares.

Field sports do not just preserve the aesthetic appearance of the landscape nor do they simply encourage landowners to maintain habitats that are of use to many other species besides game birds and foxes. Field sports are also a major economic power house within the country. Estate owners have discovered in recent years that shooting is now 'chic' with the new rich in the cities and also with rich overseas visitors who flock to the United Kingdom to enjoy the finest driven-game shooting in the world. The engine of economic demand for field sports has encouraged many landowners to plant new woods and conserve their heather-clad hills and, in parts of eastern England in particular, to farm in a more 'environmentally friendly' way, so helping game birds to breed successfully.

It is nevertheless more difficult than people would have you believe to make good money out of shooting. There are perhaps two ways of doing it. The first is obvious. If you have a really premier-division shoot, let it for a large sum of money and perhaps keep a couple of days back for your own enjoyment. The second is, if you have a big house, put up the guns and their spouses or girlfriends at anything between £150 to £250 a night per head and you should be able to make a significant profit; as you look round the table at dinner, you will find it gives you a warm feeling to count heads and work out the amount of lolly coming your way on the morrow. You may even, with luck, have some extremely amusing and interesting people staying as an added bonus.

It is not necessary to tart up the house like some nauseating hotel. Remember, your guests are enjoying a unique experience for them – staying in the proverbial stately home – so don't panic if the hot-water system blows up or some other unforeseen disaster occurs, it is all part of the 'unique country-house experience'; so relax and let your guests enjoy the 'ethnic' atmosphere. I once had a black labrador who liked to climb on the dining-room table and eat off people's plates as he wandered down it. My American guests were ecstatic. It has to be said their English hosts, from the City, did not, initially, see the joke in the same light, but they joined in the laughter when they realised the VIPs appreciated my dog's little ways.

When selling shooting you should not be over-concerned about the numbers your guns shoot, it is far more important that they fire a large number of cartridges. Many people will, when taking a day's shooting, say they want a 'two-hundred-bird' day, but they don't – or if they do, certainly shouldn't – mean it. What they should mean is that they want the opportunity to shoot two hundred birds, which is something very different indeed. You are testing your skill against theirs – your ability to show high-testing pheasants, theirs to shoot them. To avoid arguments ensure that you count the cartridges fired and, at the end of the day, if they have fired eight hundred cartridges, but only shot a hundred pheasants then they are bloody awful shots but still pay for two hundred birds.

Of course, not every shoot is run for commercial parties of guns; some are managed as syndicates and some are still kept for the owner's own private enjoyment – and some are a mixture of syndicate, private and commercial.

But it has to be said that, like any business which has expanded as rapidly as shooting has, it has its problems. The Carnarvon Report of 1992 estimated that shooting and stalking in the UK was now producing a direct expenditure of over £300 million and directly employing around 28,000 people! This is big business. To give you an idea how big, the entire the UK offshore fishing fleet only turns over around £500 million a year! But as well as direct expenditure there is the indirect aspect. All those rich Americans who travel over to the UK to shoot tend to fly first class – often on British Airways, stay a few nights in London – at a luxury hotel, kit themselves out from a very expensive London gunmaker, and so on. The Carnarvon Report put the total value of this indirect expenditure at a further £258 million, in respect of shooting, making the entire business worth over £550 million to the UK economy. Indeed, in parts of the country it is now a major contributor to the local economy, providing seasonal employment for beaters and pickers-up, as well as enabling hotels and pubs, which in the past might have closed for the winter, to be overwhelmed with guests with money to burn in their pockets.

Incidentally, the report put estimated direct expenditure on hunting at another £150 million, with a further £137 million in indirect expenditure; the figures for fishing were even larger, at £958 million and £788 million respectively, giving a grand total for amount of indirect and direct expenditure on all field sports of £1.83 billion per annum in 1992!

Inevitably, the very large amounts of money now churning through the field-sports business have led to some practices creeping in which are in danger of putting all field sports at risk. Put-and-take fishing has been with us for a long time, but in recent years some shoots have begun to practise what is virtually put-and-take shooting. Some, and it must be stressed that it is only some, and these are a comparatively small number of the total number of organised shoots in the country, are undoubtedly 'overdoing it'. Putting down too many birds on too small an acreage and shooting the same drives too often – in some cases five times or more a week – these are unacceptable practices and are rightly condemned by the vast majority of shooting people. Nevertheless they continue and threaten the entire sport; the short-term greed of some may yet bring the whole driven-shooting sport into disrepute and lead to calls for legislation to control it. Such practices are not only foolish from the point of view of the long-term public image of shooting but are bad management, pure and simple. Putting down too many birds of any variety on too small an area brings with it high risks of disease liable to wipe out large numbers of birds and leads to the commercial-shoot operator having to cancel days and lose large sums of money.

For driven-game shooting, as a commercial exercise, is not a 'no risk' business but a 'high risk' one. A big commercial shoot might sell fifty or sixty days' shooting a year and turnover around £750,000 or more per annum but it will only make money if it sells all its days. Shooting is a fixed-cost business. Nearly all the costs of running a shoot are incurred before the shooting season begins and it is only after he has sold sufficient days to cover the fixed costs that an operator can start making money. In other words, a shoot selling fifty days' shooting of, say, an average of three hundred birds, would have to sell at least thirty-five days to break even and only starts making serious money once it had sold more than forty days. A sudden down-turn in the economy leading to cancellations from people who thought they were rich in the spring and have found in the autumn, to their distress, that they are poor (as happened in the early 1990s) can lead to major losses. Similarly, outbreaks of disease in stock have a disastrous impact on the finances of a shoot.

It is in the interests of everyone who values the delights of an enjoyable day's shooting and the benefit shooting brings to the country, both environmental and economic, to try and control the greed of some of the commercial-shoot operators. In the early 1990s, the Game Conservancy Trust published a code of good conduct for the running and management of a shoot which every owner and sporting agent should read and ensure that shooting tenants and shoot organisers adhere to for the long-term good of the sport as a whole.

CHAPTER 16

The Church

Curates, long dust, will come and go
On lissom, clerical, printless toe;
And oft between the boughs is seen
The sly shade of a Rural Dean.

RUPERT BROOKE (1887–1915)

It is a lucky rural church today that boasts a curate to look after its parishioners' spiritual needs. It is only some eighty years since those lines were written but in that short timespan the Church of England has changed as much as any other of the pillars of the countryside.

English rural parish churches are surely one of the greatest glories of the countryside and can truly be said to be part of our National Heritage. Every village boasts one; some are relatively humble affairs but others are so grand as to be more like cathedrals. However, the great majority of medieval churches fall somewhere between these two extremes.

The grandeur or otherwise of a medieval church often bears witness to the riches, or lack of them, of the surrounding district during the great periods of church building, while their interiors will demonstrate whether the local 'great family' was sufficiently rich to commission grandiose monuments to their departed ancestors or not. It is one of the joys of the English parish church that sometimes a comparatively humble edifice can boast a rich interior and vice versa. Sadly, of course, most of our churches suffered from three traumatic events – the desecration unleashed by the enforcement of the reformed religion during Edward VI's reign, the triumph of the puritans under Cromwell, who completed the destruction started a hundred years earlier, and finally the equally fanatical, and often misguided, attempts at restoration undertaken by Victorian incumbents and patrons.

Churches are not the only visible signs of God's influence on rural England. What would our friends the estate agents do without that handsome Georgian property the 'Old Rectory' to offer to successful businessmen and the like? Virtually every village has a fine rectory but virtually every one is now designated 'old' since the Church Commissioners came to the regrettable conclusion, many years ago, that such large and stately buildings were no longer 'appropriate' for their parsons and, incidentally, cost far too much to maintain. The result was that after the war they sold them off in droves for relative peanuts, investing instead in building small excrescences of bungalows in prominent parts of beautiful villages to house their unfortunate clerics.

This was just one more stage in what, over a period of years, has been the Church of England's policy of looting its rural assets for the benefit of the urban church. This process still continues today. So when you wonder why you have to share a vicar with five other parishes, now you know the reason why – the assets which once supported those five incumbents have been stolen and given to more deserving causes than you poor rural folk.

What's more, it is not just the assets that have been removed to 'central control' but the appointment of the incumbent himself; this is now the province of the bishop whereas previously it used, in many instances, to be in the gift of the local squire. This 'right of patronage' was an extremely important asset. It gave the owner the right to appoint a vicar or rector to his living but – and this is imperative to remember – once the incumbent was installed he had then the 'freehold' of that living for life and there was virtually nothing the bishop or the patron could do to remove him from it till he died or gave it up. This was the reason for many of the great squire-versus-parson feuds of the eighteenth and nineteenth centuries.

This odd system of patronage allowed the Church of England to give a home to many diverse forms of worship and for the various High and Low Church sects to live in harmony under the liberal umbrella of the Church of England, secure in the knowledge that as long as a sufficient number of patrons embraced their beliefs, they would always receive their fair share of parishes to preach to.

But patronage was valuable not just because of the latitude it gave to patrons but because many livings produced exactly that, an extremely good living. In appreciation of this the eccentric Reverend Robert Hawker, vicar of Morwenstow, a relatively poor parish in Cornwall, had the following words carved above his front door:

> A house, a glebe, a pound a day,
> A pleasant place to watch and pray!
> Be true to Church – be kind to poor,
> O Minister, for evermore.

This was in 1837, when Hawker's £364 a year would have been the equivalent of more than twenty times the average income of an agricultural labourer and, in modern money, would equate to at least £30,000 a year, not taking into account what he got from farming the glebe land or letting it out.

Of course, the mixture of private patronage and highly remunerative appointments invited much abuse. Many parsons in the eighteenth and nineteenth centuries collected more than one benefice, put a poorly paid curate in to do all the tedious work, and lived handsomely on the income – a practice called pluralism, the eradication of which had, ironically, been one of Martin Luther's principal aims. Other patrons had their younger sons admitted to livings under their control at a ridiculously early age, while still others traded in them – as they could be bought and sold just like any other piece of property. For example, when my family was badly strapped for cash in 1863, they sold the living of the local parish, for one life only, to a vicar for approximately three times its annual value, which then was £400 a year.

On the credit side, it must be said that the 'good living' the church offered attracted many first-class brains and fostered diversity among incumbents which was a great strength. One wonders whether there would be any shortage of clergy today if the average stipend for a rural parish was £50,000 per annum, plus the use for life of a lovely Georgian rectory?

Even after the many reforms carried out in the nineteenth century to make pay in the church more equitable, the

Archbishop of Canterbury still received, in 1912, a salary of £15,000 a year – equivalent to over a million pounds in modern money – while many bishops got over £4,000 a year. Hardly surprising that they were called princes of the church.

But the church's influence on England's country life did not just stop at the church gate. One of the principal sources of an incumbent's income was from tithes. These were divided into great tithes and small tithes. Great tithes were levied on all things arising from the ground and subject to annual increase – corn, hay, wood. Small tithes were levied on all things nourished by the ground – the young of cattle, sheep, horses, etc. In effect, a rector owned both the great and small tithes while a vicar was only entitled to the small tithes – which neatly explains why old rectories are far grander than old vicarages.

The church justified the collection of tithes by quotes from the Old Testament such as: 'And all the tithe of the land, whether of the seed of the land, or of the fruit of the tree, is the Lord's', and, 'And concerning the tithe of the herd, or of the flock, even of whatsoever passeth under the rod, the tenth shall be holy unto the Lord' (Leviticus xxvii: 30 and 32).

None the less, it is hardly to be wondered at that by the late eighteenth century the payment of tithes had become a bone of contention between the parson and his rural flock – hence the old harvest song:

> We've cheated the parson, we'll cheat him again,
> For why should the rector have one in ten?

The remaining tithe barns stand witness to the days when the tithe was collected in kind, but in 1836 an Act of Parliament was brought in converting all payments in kind into cash payments. Tithes are now a thing of the past, having been finally abolished in 1936 when tithe owners were awarded government stock yielding three per cent redeemable in 1996!

The year 1836 marked the beginning of a series of Acts of Parliament whose aim was the gradual centralisation of authority for appointments in the bishops and the centralisation of control over assets in the Church Commissioners. So all glebe land, once the rector's or vicar's to farm or rent out as he chose, is now controlled centrally and, when planning is successfully applied for, sold off for building plots with the money going not to the parish but to the diocese. And so the pillaging of rural assets to fund urban churches goes on. Few people realised, as Act of Parliament followed Act of Parliament, that the end result of the modernisation of the Church of England would be to turn the rural church into a milch cow for the principal benefit of the urban church, but so it has turned out.

However, I sense a rebellious mood growing among rural parishes. People are beginning to ask why they should support the church outside their parish boundaries. It is a good question, too. After all, the investment decisions of the Church Commissioners have not, of late, given much cause for rejoicing. It was these paragons of financial rectitude, you may remember, who entered into a massive gamble on the property market in the 1980s. The church has always had a large proportion of its assets in property (it owns around 137,000 acres of agricultural land) and so in the 1980s' property boom its assets soared in value. So far so good; but then it forgot the lessons of the Pharaoh's dream: 'And the seven lean and ill-favoured kine do eat up the first seven fat kine' (which Joseph interpreted to mean that seven good years would be followed by seven years of famine) and instead borrowed substantial funds to invest still more heavily in the property market. The result was a disaster which the finances of the Church of England have still not recovered from.

So where might a rebellion by rural parishes lead? To unilateral declarations of independence? After all, if a parish is raising routinely some £30,000 a year it might just stop and consider that with the average stipend of a priest at £13,500 it could easily support its own dedicated parson and have some change over to put aside. It also strikes me that people might be rather more inclined to give to their local church if they knew that all the money stayed in the parish instead of being siphoned off to fund some new lunacy. Who knows, perhaps the rich banker who now lords it over the village from the Old Rectory might be prevailed upon to make a large endowment to his local church. Then they might be able to raise the stipend level to attract the best clergyman going instead of taking the bishop's choice.

It is an interesting scenario and one which may well develop over the next decade or so. Put it this way, the church has taken its rural parishioners for granted for too long – perhaps the time is ripe for the worm to turn?

But when I look at the poor state of the Church of England today I cannot but feel that a major reason for its collapse into mediocrity was amply expressed, in the mid-nineteenth century, by that towering figure from the pages of Trollope, Archdeacon Grantley, who said, on the future of the church, 'it is not the dissenters or papists we should fear, but the set of canting low-bred hypocrites who are wriggling their way in among us; men who have no fixed principles, no standard idea of religious doctrine, but who take up some popular cry, as this fellow has done . . . '

And what are all too many of the bishops and leaders of the church today if they are not 'canting low-bred hypocrites . . . men who have no fixed principles, no standard idea of religious doctrine, but who take up some popular cry . . . ?' No wonder the church has fallen so far in the esteem of its traditional supporters.

CHAPTER 17

Designations

Ever since the end of the last war, landowners have suffered a steady erosion of their freehold rights as central government has 'designated' their acres. It is ironic that those landowners who have suffered most by this creeping 'nationalisation without compensation' are exactly those landowners who have done most to conserve the environment. Now they must often curse themselves and wish they had drained the marsh, felled the 'ancient woodland', ripped out all the hedges and demolished the servant wing on their house when they had a chance.

Landowners are not alone in this regard. The 'nanny state' has spread its tentacles into virtually every nook and cranny of life in this country, to the joy of the legal profession and those who make their living by telling people what to do. It would be dishonest not to admit that much of the legislation introduced over the last eighty-odd years has been provoked by various people, some landowners included, ruthlessly pursuing profit in total disregard of aesthetic or moral considerations. That these people were a minority, in some cases a tiny one, makes no difference; it is often said that 'good cases make bad laws'. So a farmer ripping out hedges in East Anglia to make a field of a hundred acres in extent will cause regulations to be brought in that will stop a farmer in Devon removing a hedge to make a five-acre field into a ten-acre one; the wholesale planting up of the Flow Country in Caithness with Sitka spruce as a tax dodge for private investors generates reform of the entire forestry grants and tax regime, to the detriment of thousands of responsible woodland owners. In other words, one bad apple can, because of the bad publicity it attracts, cause immeasurable harm to all people operating in the same field, whether it be in agriculture or any other profession or business.

The rot started with the setting up of the National Parks after the last war. This attempt to safeguard England's remaining 'wild areas' by designating them 'National Parks', subject to special planning considerations, was well meaning in its aim and has – in part – succeeded. The failing of the National Parks has been, ironically, as a result of their success – too many people are now flocking to the areas, putting too much pressure on the infrastructure of the parks and on land which was never designed to cope with the massed tramp of heavily shod feet over its ancient pathways. Watching walkers on the hills I often wonder why they have to dress as though they were about to scale some mountain peak, and I reflect on the type of mind which can criticise a farmer for 'ruining' the view by storing his silage in black plastic bags without realising that the bright yellow, red or blue waterproof with which its own body is adorned is a far greater blot on the landscape.

Actually the National Parks were not as new a concept in England as is sometimes made out. The father of conservation in England was none other than William the Conqueror, who after the conquest caused many areas of land to be 'afforested'. He cleared them of all people and preserved them strictly, via draconian forest laws. The New Forest in Hampshire is one of his principal legacies.

But the National Parks were only the start of a programme of 'designation' which, like a stone rolling down the hill, has gathered increasing momentum as the years have gone by. The spread of statutory designations over the countryside can be illustrated by the following table.

Admittedly these areas are not all exclusive. In other words, land designated an SSSI may well be within a National Park and it is feasible that an SSSI is also a NVZ and is in a AONB. However, when all is said and done the percentage of land in the UK falling under one form or other of the above designations must be around a third. I do wonder at the amount of land scientists seem to require – am I alone in thinking that at 6.5% of the total rural acreage of the UK they are becoming a little greedy? If the rate of growth continues in this particular form of designation (and at the time of writing it shows no signs of slowing) we shall soon

Designation	Area in hectares	Percentage of rural land
Green Belts	1,550,000	12.0%
Areas of Outstanding Natural Beauty (AONB)	2,040,000	13.0%
National Parks	1,360,000	9.0%
Sites of Special Scientific Interest (SSSI)	975,000	6.5%
Nitrate Vulnerable Zones (provisional) (NVZ)	635,000	4.2%
Total	6,560,000	44.7%

Source: CLA 1997

have to rename SSSIs and call them instead Sites of Common Scientific Interest (SCSI).

The list is far from exhaustive, it does not include, for instance, areas of ancient woodland, or Heritage coastline, nor does it include other designations such as Environmentally Sensitive Areas (ESA) or Less Favoured Areas (LFA). Admittedly, ESAs and LFAs are less to do with planning and control and more concerned with provision of grants and subsidies to those lucky enough to live within their boundaries.

The good news for those in the designation business, as I write, is that we are about to have two new ones thrust upon us, courtesy of Brussels. These exciting new entrants to the field are called Special Protection Areas (SPAs), which have arisen because of the EU Birds Directive, and Special Areas of Conservation (SACs), which are a result of the EU Habitats directive. At present it is not clear whether SPAs will replace existing SSSIs or whether, as seems more likely, SSSIs will continue and a few will be selected to boast the additional honour of being an SPA or an SAC.

The SAC designation carries a potentially nasty sting in its tail in that though the designation may actually only apply to, say, a ten-acre site, controls on farming practices, etc. may be enforced on adjacent land as well.

Where will it all end? Probably not until every last acre in the UK has been surveyed and designated, and a whole host of bodies and bureaucrats have grown up to administer the procedures, etc. which designation obviously entails, all at enormous cost to the taxpayer. It is a boom industry and, like ever other industry, Parkinson's law will apply: 'Work expands to fill the time available for its completion.' Except, in this case, land designations will expand to justify the employment of yet more graduates in environmental studies, driving around the countryside in smart new Land-Rovers.

Landowners must learn to live with these designations just as owners of listed buildings have learnt to live with the planning controls over their properties. Life is not all bad and many may find that grants are available as a result of their land being designated – indeed some owners of grouse moors are already finding, to their surprise and joy, that grants can now be got for heather improvement and regeneration.

CHAPTER 18

The Future

What of the future? Well it is true to say that the future of estates and big houses looks brighter today than at any time since 1875. Partly this is due to rarity value. There are simply too few of us left for there to be any political capital to be made out of driving the remainder of us to extinction. It is a maxim that the British public, and its government, only wakes up to a disaster when it has nearly destroyed something of value, and then rushes around like a flock of headless chickens trying to save what remains. The heritage industry is awash with examples of this peculiar trait.

It was in just such a way that planners presided over the destruction of town centre after town centre in the post-war period and then suddenly charged around and slapped conservation orders on the few which were as yet not wrecked. Why it took them so long to realise the enormous damage they were doing is a mystery to anyone but a town planner.

So with the number of estates in England and Wales reduced to around twelve hundred, a number still dwindling, I think that we are relatively safe from direct attack from politicians. Scotland, of course, is another matter. Soon it will boast a directly elected assembly with powers, among others, of tax raising; it will be interesting to see how they exercise them. In these circumstances, I am not as sanguine on the future in Scotland as in England and Wales. A cursory reading of the Scottish press will show that there is a wealth of ignorance and prejudice concerning the role and responsibilities of landowners north of the border, specific-ally 'absentee landowners'. Perhaps the time is now ripe for some serious assessment to be made of the enormous amount of money injected into the economy of the Highlands and Islands by this much maligned species of individual over the last hundred years or so. Sadly I suspect that a Lowlands-dominated assembly may view landowners as easy prey to satisfy the bloodlust of their more rabid constituents, regardless of the long-term effect on the economy of the Highlands.

I suspect that in the event most future attacks on landowners in England and Wales, as well as in Scotland, will be of an indirect nature. The fog of officialdom will, I am convinced, creep further into the interstices of country life as politicians, congratulating themselves on having 'saved' some of 'our heritage', determine to ensure that the people who actually saved it are no longer empowered to do anything with it without groping their way through a baffling bureaucratic maze. Gradually the cult of planning and designation will extend to the whole countryside as Areas of Outstanding Natural Beauty, National Parks, Environmentally Sensitive Areas or Sites of Special Scientific Interest, Nitrate Sensitive Areas, Ancient Woodlands and Heritage Coastlines all expand their areas and responsibilities, and, no doubt, several new designations yet to be dreamed up come into existence. The determination of urban man to meddle in the affairs of the countryside and to try to mould it into the image of what he considers it should be like will continue to strengthen; in other words, the 'Disneyfication' of rural Britain for the benefit of the townies will carry on and the time cannot be to far off when countrymen are offered grants to dress in smocks and chew straw to project a correct rural image – although this might raise an outcry that 'ethnic minorities' are insufficiently represented in rural Britain. In fact, there is already an organisation called the Black Environment Network (BEN) dedicated to 'the promotion of the use of the countryside as a leisure resource by ethnic minority groups'. The time is fast approaching when an orchestrated campaign will be launched to ensure that the population of Britain's rural villages reflect the 'multi-cultural society'. Paradoxically I suspect that the people who will be foremost in propounding this nonsense will be the same ones who are trying to insist that no tree be planted which does not originate from racially pure 'native' stock. There seems to me to be an anomaly here!

As such urban meddling increases, so jobs in the country

connected with the various bodies appointed to rule rural Britain will multiply until environmental or countryside 'officers' will, in their various guises, outnumber traditional farmers, farmworkers, foresters, gamekeepers and the like, just as today there are more people employed by Social Services than there are servicemen in the UK's armed forces. It will of course be imperative that all employees of such bodies are graduates of one of the many fatuous environmental and conservationist courses run at Britain's universities and that they proudly boast the title of 'officer', which is surely one of the most devalued words in the English language.

Another legacy of urban interference is the paranoia whipped up by the press and ignorant politicians from time to time on 'food safety'. There are bound to be more 'scare' stories in the years ahead, if only for the reason that they make good copy and newspapers and television companies can always find some scientist to support the latest scare and give credence to it. In fact, logic suggests there will be many more food scares for two reasons. First, ironically, because food is simply getting 'safer'. Let me explain. Those of us brought up on unpasteurised milk and good old-fashioned food built up a level of immunity against many germs and diseases. As everything becomes 'debugged' by law these days, so the modern child builds up no such levels of resistance; the end result is that he is that much more vulnerable to the odd germ so that when he does swallow one, by mistake, the result is likely to be that much more devastating. Second, the high cost of imposing strict food-hygiene regulations means, in effect, that the number of food processors will be very much reduced (as has already happened in the case of abattoirs, whose numbers have diminished steeply) under the weight of regulation; the concentration of food processing in a few large centres will mean that if a 'bug' does begin to breed in one of these factories it will adversely affect a very large segment of the population.

As for food retailing, inevitably the smaller greengrocer, butcher, etc. will continue to be squeezed by the large supermarkets, who jump with joy at every regulation, knowing that it will drive yet more small businesses to the wall and give them even greater domination of their market.

   That such domination is 'good' for the consumer is one of
those fallacies which have taken hold. As I write in 1998 we have
seen the price of milk paid to a farmer fall by twenty per cent in
the past year, but not a penny of that saving in raw-material cost
has been passed on to the end user. It is the same story with all
farm products – if the price falls the supermarkets increase their
profit margins and seldom if ever pass it on to the consumer in
reduced prices.
   But perhaps I am too gloomy and perhaps the thousands who
attended the Countryside Rally in June 1997 and the 280,000 who
marched through London peacefully in the spring of 1998 will
have persuaded politicians to pause and think again.

What of the current state of the rural economy? I have touched
on the problems in preceding chapters, but in the last analysis I
am a bull of both farming and forestry, in the long term that is. I
foresee a boom in commodities brought about by the emergence
of China and, perhaps, India as major economic powers. In the
short to medium term, however, things look like getting quite
rough in the agricultural sector and I expect to see farms
continuing to get larger and more efficient in order to survive.
Subsidies from the CAP will become less productivity driven and
more and more orientated towards acreage payments, with, I
suspect, a strong built-in bias against large farmers in the form
of a limit on the amount of subsidy capable of being received by
any one farmer.
   In the long term prospects look good, and I see the day when
world prices will reach such heights that food exports from the
EU will be restricted in an attempt to hold down prices to the EU
consumer.
   It must be the same with rural property generally. The future
must look good. We are conscious of being in the middle of what
tomorrow's schoolchildren will possibly call the Communications
Revolution; they will be forced to sit through hours of boring
lessons learning about it and how it affected the lives of ordinary
people, just like our generation had to learn about the Industrial
Revolution.
   The Industrial Revolution, of course, sucked labour and capital

out of the countryside to feed its insatiable demands, and destroyed small rural cottage industries in the process. It would seem logical that the Communications Revolution may have the reverse effect – it may suck people and capital out of smelly towns and back into rural Britain and once again make cottage industries possible. Already there are signs that this is happening in a small way, and I expect that over the next twenty years this move will gather pace and those with nice properties to let in beautiful parts of the country will reap the benefit. With any luck the revolution will arrive in time to save many redundant eighteenth- and nineteenth-century farm buildings from falling down. On the debit side the cost of rural housing is likely to continue to rise in real terms, causing shortages of affordable rural housing even to the 'native' population. However as businesses move out of the Home Counties, wage rates and job opportunities will rise in rural areas. The increasing number of 'immigrants' to the countryside will reinforce old hostilities as newly settled townies attempt to force their urban attitudes to life on the resentful native population. There is a need for true countrymen to be protected as a distinct 'ethnic minority', and organisations dedicated to looking after rural interests must give this some thought as a matter of urgency.

Landowning is all about taking the long view, we must leave short-termism for those who work in industry and the City. Looking forward fifty years, I think we can feel optimistic that things have at last come right for us, accepting there may be a temporary agricultural recession within the immediate future. Farming will be a very different ball-game over the next quarter-century than it has been over the last twenty-five years. It will far more resemble the historic farming industry, with the gradual removal of the feather bed of guaranteed prices and increasing exposure to the rough world of roller-coaster commodity prices. In other words, farmers and landowners will have to learn to live in a 'boom or bust' environment. A drought in China or the Midwest of the USA will be just as important to their financial wellbeing as decisions made in Brussels.

A further word about global warming, the current concern of environmentalists everywhere. According to some commentators, it will mean that we will be producing fine wines and growing olive trees in the UK within twenty-five years. Personally, I think that this is balls. That is not to say that I believe our climate will never change – it will and it does. The last ice age ended only twelve thousand years ago and as recently as the seventeenth century the Thames in London froze solid enough for frost fairs to held on the river, and the sea froze between Iceland and the Faroe Islands.

Amusingly, environmentalists who agree that we are going to be affected by global warming disagree about the outcome. One school of thought predicts the UK will enjoy the sort of climate France now has in the Loire Valley, while the opposition considers that higher world temperatures will cause ice to melt at the North Pole and the resulting cold water flowing south will force the Gulf Stream to change course; this would mean our climate would more resemble that of southern Norway than that of southern France.

There is a third school of thought that says this whole global-warming debate has been invented by environmentalists in order to justify spending large sums of taxpayers' money on going to exotic locations for 'world conferences' and on endless research projects. Being a cynic, I subscribe to this theory.

As for the future of large country houses, that too looks good. The 'industrial revolution' will continue to invent and perfect devices for making living in such houses easier and less labour intensive, while the current 'communications revolution' will – in the long term – provide uses for many redundant outbuildings. Country houses and estates are, by definition, now in very limited supply while, I suspect, the number of people who would like to own one and have the wherewithal to do so is continuing to grow. I also discern encouraging signs of a resurgence of the rental market in large houses. Back in the eighteenth, nineteenth and early twentieth centuries, it was common if a family had fallen on hard times for them to let their house for a period until their finances recovered. Already owners of reasonably sized properties with an hour or so of London are cashing in on this idea as an alternative to selling their properties. Hardly surprising, as renting can be a good deal for both parties: on the one hand, the owner retains title and the option to move back in at the end of the tenancy, while picking up a large rent, often in the region of fifty to seventy thousand pounds a year; on the other hand, the tenant has the use and enjoyment of a stately home for a fraction of the cost of buying one.

Those owners who are involved, or tempted to become involved, in the much trumpeted 'leisure revolution' should tread carefully. The public will become increasingly demanding regarding the quality and variety of attractions on offer, and this will inevitably lead to an ever higher level of investment in what will become a very competitive market, dominated by professional companies with deep pockets.

In short, those of us who own estates and are used to playing the long game will reflect on our good fortune to have had fathers and grandfathers and great-grandfathers who somehow managed to weather the appallingly turbulent years between 1875 and 1979.